Parental
Child-Stealing

Parental Child-Stealing

Michael W. Agopian
California Lutheran College

LexingtonBooks
D.C. Heath and Company
Lexington, Massachusetts
Toronto

Library of Congress Cataloging in Publication Data

Agopian, Michael
    Parental child-stealing.

    Bibliography: p.
    Includes index.
    1. Kidnapping, Parental-United States. I. Title.
HV6598.A46   364.1'54   80-8591
ISBN 0-669-04152-1   AACR2

Published simultaneously in Canada

Printed in the United States of America

International Standard Book Number: 0-669-04152-1

Library of Congress Catalog Card Number: 80-8591

For Gil Geis,
Friend, Mentor, and Inspiration

Contents

List of Tables

Foreword

Few persons who commit criminal acts do so for other than what they regard as admirable reasons. The shoplifter points out that he is merely reclaiming a bit of the exorbitant profits that the supermarket or department store obtains through mulcting the public. Besides, the merchandise was displayed deliberately to tempt and tantalize. Anyway, the stolen goods undoubtedly are covered by insurance, and the store probably will cheat the insurance company by inflating its claim for losses.

Even murderers often feel supremely self-righteous about what they have done. Interrogating detectives play upon this psychology. "It's amazing," the detectives will say to the man who has hacked his wife to bits, "that you were able to put up with somebody like her for all these years." Sympathetically, they observe, "Anybody else probably would've killed her a long time ago. You must be some kind of a saint."

The ax-murderer, pleased that his virtues are truly appreciated, may now modestly admit what he has done, perhaps anticipating further praise for his forebearance over the years. After all, given the provocation he believes he endured, he might well have done her in in a much more brutal manner.

Parental child-stealers are not different from other persons who violate the law. They want to believe that what they have done was in the best interests of all concerned, or, at least, all those who have decent motives. They are in a better position to justify their actions than most criminal offenders because as parents they clearly have a sanctioned and legitimate interest in the welfare of their children. A recent newspaper story detailing several cases of fathers who "reclaimed" their children is set out under the headline: "Fathers Tell How Love for Children Drove Them to Break Law". One father is quoted as mournfully observing, "I know I've messed up and made some mistakes, but I just wanted to be with my little girl." The out-in-the-cold parent characteristically believes that his child will do better under his care than that of his former mate who, he may insist, among other things, is squandering his hard-earned support payments on herself and her new boyfriend and is thereby depriving the child of its due. And, of course, the exposure of the malleable child to the "immoral" behavior of the parent with court-granted custody is intolerable. There are, besides these, an entire range of justifications that underlie attempts by divorced and separated parents to regain control of their children. Some of these beliefs undoubtedly are accurate appraisals of the situation—in some cases a child assuredly will be better off with the parent who "steals" him.

As yet, we do not have satisfactory information about the consequences of child-stealing on the persons involved, that is, each of the parents and the child or children. In a recent editorial headed "When Parents Steal Kids," the *New York Times* (13 October 1980) claimed that "[a]lthough the children are rarely injured physically, virtually all youngsters under five suffer psychological damage." The source for this conclusion is not indicated, and the accuracy of the observation seems arguable. In some instances, child-stealing undoubtedly is frightening and traumatic for youngsters, particularly since it is apt to disrupt their routine and expectations. On the other hand, the behavior may be regarded as a testament of parental concern, and, thereby, provide a measure of flattering attention. It also could add excitement and novelty to an otherwise mundane existence. Many of the parents who take their children go to great pains to ingratiate themselves with the youngsters. They may, at least for a time, provide the kind of holiday merriment that so often angers a parent who has day-to-day child-care responsibilities and observes the weekend custodian entertaining the child royally during brief visitation spans. These are the kinds of research data that only further study can supply. It seems apparent that the history of the parental relationship; the kind of person the child is; the ingredients of the event during which the parent takes illegal custody of the child; the details of the subsequent situation, including living arrangements, affectional components, school experiences; and a host of other matters, all have an important bearing on the sequelae for the participants in the child-stealing.

This book by Michael Agopian is a pioneering scholarly inventory of the dimensions of child-stealing. It examines the behavior as it occurs in Los Angeles, a city where such acts, as so many other forms of human enterprise, seem to be the precursor of trends that shortly will manifest themselves elsewhere in the United States. Agopian reviews all the cases in which a parent denied custody of his or her own child took the child away from the law-designated custodian. The ninety-one instances that fell into this category, during the initial year of operation of a California statute that significantly tightened up the definition and control of child-stealing, provide a study group that allows a thorough consideration of the demographics and dynamics of child-stealing.

I do not want to anticipate the important findings that the book sets out, except to focus on one that particularly caught my attention. Child-stealing, Agopian found, was perpetrated by men in 71 percent of the cases studied and by women in the remaining 29 percent. Los Angeles court officials have never made a count of the distribution of custody orders in terms of whether the child was awarded to the mother or to the father; besides, many divorced couples make their own arrangements, and, unless disputed, these do not become court business. But the officials are rather certain, as I am, that men do not receive child custody decrees in nearly as many as 29 percent of the divorce cases in the country. Child-stealing, then, disproportionately involves women who "normally" might have been expected to get custody, but who did not. They steal from men who, against; the averages, were favored by the court. These figures, it seems to me, provide considerable insight into forces that prompt child-stealing. Being deprived of custody must be particularly devastating for many women since it goes against role expectations and demands. The situation probably exposes them to a considerable amount of peer scorn. The situation may be evocative of a strong need to regain the child they believe rightfully belongs to them—a child they think they can better tend than the man to whom it was awarded by the courts.

Similar kinds of impulses probably play a part in shaping the acts of men who retake their children from their former wives. It is likely that the amount of child-stealing in the United States has increased with changes in sex roles and definitions. In the past, men expected and accepted the loss of regular communication with their children as part of the institutionalized aspect of divorce. They have learned that this no longer need be the case, that they too can perform satisfactorily as a single parent, and that they may have as much right to their child as its mother does. What is made possible and feasible, but then is officially disallowed, can then be interpreted as a stinging deprivation. When something is lost that its former possessor believes ought to be his, the stage is set for attempts at retrieval, though such attempts may violate legal dictates.

Conversely, of course, women have been learning—and the lesson has been heeded (aided by economic conditions)—that they should enter the marketplace competitively with men. For some, this has led to combined child-rearing, family-tending, and occupational demands. For others, the result has been a sharing of domestic chores; and, for still others, the economic and social appeals of their lives in the marketplace have led to abandonment of child and husband. What is notable is that the social scene today is such that either parent can find self-justification for the assumption that he or she more reasonably ought to have control of the child that jointly was parented before the dissolution of the marriage. The relationship between views of sex roles and characteristics of child-stealing remains a key realm for detailed investigation.

It is noteworthy, in this context, that the best known child-custody dispute—that set forth in the biblical story depicting Solomon's wisdom (1 Kings 3:16-28)—involved not a father and a mother arguing over their child, but, rather, two mothers who sought an impartial determination of which of them was the lawful custodian of a child. In biblical times, as until very recent years, paternal investment with parenting was not so prescriptive; the biblical story undoubtedly would have been less compelling had one of the disputants been the child's father contesting the rights of its mother.

The protagonists in the Solomon story, it may be recalled, were two harlots. Both of the women had been delivered of a child at the same time; three days later one of them smothered her own infant to death by inadvertently rolling upon it while she slept. The distraught woman substituted her own dead child for the live infant of the other mother. Solomon's task was to determine which one truly was the parent of the surviving infant. He requested a sword and threatened to sever the child into two parts, giving half to one woman and half to the other. When one of the women protested, telling the king that she would agree to have the other take the child rather than to see it killed, Solomon was certain that he had found the true mother. His judicial achievement, the Bible tells us, led all Israel to fear the King for "they saw that the wisdom of God was in him, to do justice." For us, the story illustrates the intense personal and social preferences and pressures that demand of a parent that it stay in close and continuing contact with its offspring.

Parallels to the story of Solomon can be located in the folklore of virtually all early Eastern peoples. In Indian mythology, for instance, the child in dispute in a similar tale is subjected to a tug-of-war in which the actual mother is identified only when she abandons the struggle. What distinguishes the Solomon story is that it represents the first time in the Bible that the details of a juridical resolution of a dispute are set forth. Each claimant presents her case, and an impartial adjudicator then resolves the issue. But the story also symbolizes the kind of event that might engage emotions and demand wisdom. It quickly captured contemporary imaginations, and a painting depicting the biblical story which was discovered in the ruins of Pompeii can be seen today in the Museum in Naples.

Besides the role imperatives involved in the genesis of child-stealing occurrences, there also are structural conditions that play into the behavior, as Agopian's study illustrates. In England, for instance, child-stealing is uncommon; those I asked about it could tell stories in which daft old women stole someone else's child from a pram and then treated the infant as if it were their own. It is believed that child-stealing is rare in England because there are fewer places where the child can be hidden, and there are not the extradition barriers that prevail when a child is taken across state borders in the United States. In addition, American jurisdictions may take it upon themselves to redetermine the legal custody status of a child and may decide, for instance, that the parent denied custody in California is entitled to such custody in Louisiana. The stage then is set for a continuing sequence of counter-stealings, much like the ongoing medieval vendettas.

The Federal Parental Kidnaping Prevention Act of 1980 may go some way toward ameloirating some of the structural conditions that encourage child-stealing. The measure requires all states to honor the child-custody decisions of other states, and, thus, removes the earlier possibility offered by a number of jurisdictions to reexamine the custody issue. A second provision of the statute expands the use of the federal parent locator service to pursue persons suspected of having wrongly seized their children. The locator uses address records of the Internal Revenue Service, Social Security, and other agencies to track down parents who are delinquent in making child-support payments. Two arguments, one pragmatic, the other philosophical, can be made against this provision of the federal bill. First, there is some doubt that the locator program would be of much use since child-stealing parents can avoid its snares without much difficulty; besides, the available information tends to be outdated. In the philosophical realm, there are serious objections to the provision on the ground that it constitutes an unwarranted invasion of personal privacy.

The third major clause in the federal law enlists the Federal Bureau of Investigation through use of the Fugitive Felon Act in efforts to locate a child-stealing parent for whom a state has issued an arrest warrant.

Child-stealing basically is a consequence of an immutable arithmetic fact. If parents of a child separate, only one—or neither—will be able to have the child under its care most of the time. The parents may evenly—or almost evenly—divide the custody, but that arrangement will only be satisfactory if the participants perceive it as preeminently fair. Such a strict calculation of custody time, indeed, may exacerbate conditions since it establishes a basis for continuous contact between the parents.

How such matters might best be resolved, how custody might fairly be determined, and how its consequences might decently be accepted are formidable issues that become increasingly important as divorce rates rise. Michael Agopian's thorough examination of cases of parental child-stealing offers a rich mine of information on the ingredients of a phenomenon that may be taken to epitomize contemporary relationships.

Gilbert Geis
Program in Social Ecology
University of California

Preface

One of the most complex forms of criminal behavior is that which concerns offenses involving family members. They are especially difficult to understand because of the intimate relationship between the parties, the private environment in which they are perpetrated, and the vast array of motivations which induce them. Crimes such as wife-beating and child abuse depict the distinctive nature of violence and suffering inflicted by family members. These more visible types of domestic crime generally cease with divorce. But a new and growing family crime has developed as a repercussion of the divorce process. Children of divorce now face an increasing chance of being abducted by the parent who loses custody following the breakup of a marriage.

Although it is increasingly common, divorce remains a battle that produces winners and losers. Ex-spouses who wage combat over an equitable division of property are now staunchly fighting to retain custody of the child. The hostility of divorce frequently is channeled into the ultimate battle of the war between ex-spouses—the struggle to retain custody of the child.

Three years ago I addressed a national commission investigating parental child-stealing. I vividly recall my conversations afterward with parents whose children had been abducted. The frustration and sorrow expressed by those parents was wrenching. They expressed disbelief at the confusion within the laws, the ease with which offenders circumvent authorities, the limitations of police agencies in assisting them, and the blatant disregard for the law frequently exhibited by offenders on those rare occasions when they would contact the custodial parent. That day I observed how parental child-snatching becomes a traumatic and shattering event for the abducted child and especially for the parent now searching for his or her child. The pain and chaos that pervades the life of a parent who has lost a child was manifest.

Child-stealing breeds a hopelessness that tests even the most optimistic of persons. It becomes a consuming experience that taps the energy, faith, and financial resources of parents and, frequently, their relatives. The experience is a shadow that stalks custodial parents. It lingers and permeates their daily actions. As one custodial parent who had searched for her son for over a year explained to me, "I stared at every young boy walking down the street thinking if that could be Robbie. When passing a school I look into the school yard wondering if he could be in that crowd. I think to myself, 'What is he doing? How is he cared for? And why would my ex-husband do this to me?' But it's hardest during the holidays. That's when I miss him most." Such a reaction is blanketed in the deep sorrow and continued anguish custodial parents endure.

In the past two years an enormous ground swell of sentiment and interest has developed over parental child-stealing. The media is now reporting and updating developments relating to parental child-abductions. Legislation at the federal and state levels is being initiated to attack the problem. International agreements are being drafted. Judges are discarding deeply entrenched biases against fathers as suitable custodial parents. More judges are accepting the challenge to create equitable and functional custody awards. There remains, however, a mammoth void of knowledge to guide public policy and understanding in the prevention of parental child-stealing. It is with a desire to illuminate this debilitating and unusual human problem and, thus, to effect change that the present work was designed. Parental child-thefts pose an extraordinary challenge that demands our creativity, dedication, and resources.

This book explores the nature and dimensions of the abduction of children by parents. It examines the adjudication of cases, sketches a portrait of individuals engaging in this activity, and details the situational and circumstantial ingredients of the crime process. It strives to assess with compassion and equity the persons in and characteristics of this tangled web of relations that often follows divorce.

The fact that the Los Angeles County District Attorney's Office provided assistance and information for this research does not indicate the concurrence of the district attorney in the statements or conclusions contained within the study.

Acknowledgments

I am indebted to a number of individuals for their assistance during the course of this study. Gretchen Anderson contributed valuable guidance and organizational perspective during the entire project. I owe a special debt of gratitute to Gretchen for her motivation and friendship during the past years. Gilbert Geis provided important direction for and careful review of each component of the research. His wisdom and support pervades this endeavor. I thank Rod McKenzie for his continued interest in the project and his careful critiques of an earlier version of the manuscript.

Many individuals in the Los Angeles County District Attorney's Office contributed to this project. I am sincerely grateful to District Attorney John Van de Kamp and Assistant District Attorney Johnnie Cochran for authorizing the research. Deputy District Attorney Martin Oghigian spent many hours explaining and debating legal and procedural aspects relating to parental child-stealing. His assistance and friendship is deeply appreciated. Paul Newman patiently and conscientiously guided the review of case records and made the data collection process more pleasant than expected. Yvonne Estrada, Robert Altman, Larry Morrison, and many other individuals within the district attorney's office graciously contributed to this study.

I also want to express my appreciation to former Assemblyman Michael Antonovich who provided valuable material regarding the law and parental child-stealing. Lee Baca of the Los Angeles County Sheriff's Department, Steve Hodel of the Los Angeles Police Department, and Dent Wheeler of the Glendale Police Department kindly aided in locating elusive case material.

Frances Coles was subjected to my intemperate preoccupation with parental child-stealing during the past two years. I thank her for many valuable suggestions and for her patience during various stages of the research. Stephanie Parks turned ragged notes into clean preliminary drafts, and Jane Gray completed an excellent job of typing the final manuscript. Margaret Zusky was a knowledgeable and encouraging editor.

Most important, I am especially indebted to my parents, John and Rose Agopian, for their support, patience, and love.

Parental
Child-Stealing

1 A Study of Parental Child-Stealing

Crime conjures a repulsive yet peculiarly fascinating image. Crime between family members, however, presents an especially intriguing vision into an area of human behavior which has until very recently remained unexplored. As family relations are more deeply probed, it is becoming evident that interactions among family members are increasingly perilous and unstable. The dissolution of a marriage was usually considered to be a way of insuring family members against future episodes of violence.

Of the many changes the fragile American family has recently experienced, perhaps the most dramatic is the increasing number of marriages ending in divorce. Although it is almost commonplace, individuals appear to be experiencing greater difficulties in dealing with the new pressures, roles, and relationships created by divorce. The change and adjustments faced by family members undergoing divorce has spawned a new and serious family crime. With the domestic war settled by divorce, increasing numbers of ex-spouses are now waging the final battle of the marital war over custody of the children. Historically, children have been the real losers in divorce, but they now have become the prized possession to be batted about between divorcing parents. An unusual consequence of the burgeoning number of ex-spouses fighting over custody of their children is the abduction of a child by a parent. Parental child-stealing is the act of a parent abducting or detaining a child from the custodial parent in violation of a custody decree. It may occur during a separation prior to a divorce action or following a divorce.

Contact with a child has been a fundamental right of parents. Only in rare instances have courts deprived a parent of access to his child. These instances are usually based on clear evidence that the child will be in physical danger if placed in the parent's custody. The child's right to contact with his parents must also be preserved. The wishes of children affected by divorce, and especially of those who are the subject of embittered custody disputes, are commonly overlooked.

Parental child-stealing disrupts the orderly process whereby the control of children following a divorce is established. This self-help method of resolving custody disputes creates havoc for abducted children and suffering for the custodial parent. It frustrates the legal process designed to provide order and stability for marriages with minor children that end in divorce.

1

The objective of this work is to examine the nature and patterns of parental child-stealing. This examination is based on cases screened for prosecution by the Los Angeles County District Attorney's Office during the initial year following special legislation in California banning such activity—July 1, 1977 to June 30, 1978.

The study emphasizes the drama and complexity of the crime and analyzes characteristics of the offenders, custodial parents, and abducted children. It also describes situational and circumstantial aspects of the offense. The present research forsakes a global conception of crime and strives toward an analysis of the nature of one specific crime. It requires placing an analytical microscope upon the particular offense to understand the context in which the crime was committed and the patterns and particular individuals involved in such activity. This approach seeks, first, to identify those situations which increase the possibility that such a crime will be committed, and, second, to uncover data revealing important relationships of attributes and variables. Such a study of parental child-stealing may provide an objective body of information surrounding the crime and its participants.

Analysis of a particular type of crime and of the offenders and victims is relatively rare in criminology although the orientation has been applied to crimes such as homicide,[1] forcible rape,[2] and robbery.[3] By focusing upon one specific type of criminal activity, the present work recognizes the caution echoed by Morris:

> Perhaps it is time we faced the fact that the generally used concept of "crime" is altogether too broad to be of much use to the serious investigators of criminal behavior. . . . I am suggesting that if we are to get on with the business of learning to deal more effectively with crime, we had better stop talking about crime and begin to identify and study with as much care and thoroughness as is possible the nature and workings of the significant factors essential to each type of criminal behavior.[4]

Because no data exists about the nature of parental child-stealing, descriptive information pointing to important relationships between variables and social attributes can provide a basis for assessing the dynamics of this activity. Such a perspective can uncover patterns, interlinkages, and ingredients of the crime overlooked or falsely attributed and provide a foundation for future research.

A proper understanding of the nature of parental child-stealing demands the construction of a detailed order among inherent events and social factors. In addition to offenders and victims, it is necessary to study the primary factors of the situation under which the abductions occurred and the various social characteristics of the participants involved in order to unravel the social fabric of parental child-stealing.

No formal study as yet exists to develop propositions for confirmation regarding parental child-stealing. From extensive interviews with prosecutors[5] and analyses of numerous case accounts,[6] one may assume that the crimes of parental child-stealing contain discernible uniformities and unique characteristics. On the basis of these assumptions and a preliminary review of data contained within district attorney case records, answers to important questions about parental child-stealing are sought in the present study.

The study attempts to examine the nature of parental child-stealing by describing three dimensions of the crime: first, the adjudication of cases reviewed by the district attorney; second, the participants involved—offender, custodial parent, and abducted child; and, third, the temporal, spatial, situational, and circumstantial elements surrounding the crime.

The court disposition of parental child-stealing cases screened by the district attorney for prosecution is an important concern in the analysis of the crime. Such data may help assess the vigor and determination with which child-stealing cases are prosecuted. Disposition information may also aid in determining whether courts and prosecutors apply "selective inattention" to this complex and unique family crime. What proportion of parental child-stealing offenses are filed for prosecution? What number are rejected and for what reasons? How many cases are unsolved with the offender and child unlocated? With an extensive relationship between offender and custodial parent, how frequently do custodial parents refuse to prosecute? Is parental child-stealing characterized by the custodial parent filing charges with the sole intent to recover the child and later withdrawing from prosecution? Do parental child-stealing cases involve trials, pleas, dismissals, or some form of charge negotiation? Is extradition frequent for prosecution, and what amount of bail is usually involved? Finally, what type of sentence is imposed upon individuals convicted of parental child-stealing?

It will be of interest to study what the differences are between offenders and custodial parents. Do important demarcations exist between offenders and custodial parents with regard to sex, race, age, and employment? Knowledge of the marital status of offenders and custodial parents should be valuable in understanding parental child-stealing. Are the parties divorced, separated prior to divorce proceedings, or presently married but unable to agree upon the custody of a child? How frequently are children abducted from cohabitation relationships? Are interracial relationships frequent in parental child-stealing cases? What type of child is abducted by a parent? Are stolen children usually infants, or are adolescents also the target of offending parents? Are individual children stolen, or are multiple siblings abducted? The final and, perhaps, important aspect of studying parental child-stealing relates to its outcome—how frequently are children located or returned when they are the target of child-thefts?

Other questions are concerned with the time and space patterns of parental child-stealing. Do child-thefts occur more frequently during certain time periods, days of the week, or seasons of the year? Parental child-stealing might be assumed to be a weekend or summer type of crime. The abduction might take the form of an extension of the court-prescribed weekend visitation period or the offender's refusal to return the child after a summer-long visit. Because the opportunity to snatch the child is essential, incorporating the crime into the court-ordered visitation period would insure easy access to the child and provide a period for the offender to flee. Or does the offender utilize a surprise abduction unrelated to the visitation period, thereby forsaking a buffer period to aid concealment?

It is rare for criminologists to study the actual site of the crime. Where did the abduction occur? In a surprise abduction, can we expect the child-theft to occur in an open space or on a desolate street while the child is in transit, perhaps to school or play? But if the child-theft is incorporated into the visitation period, it should follow that the victim's residence will be the site of the crime. The ecology of parental child-stealing should provide information useful to parents and law enforcement personnel in creating a program to reduce child-thefts and insure that the intentions of custody orders are maintained.

If important sex, race, age, and other basic demographic differences or patterns are manifested in parental child-stealing, do they persist when essential situational and circumstantial factors of the crime are examined? The way in which the crime is carried out—the modus operandi—and the behavior of the offender and custodial parent during the crime may demonstrate key trends and patterns. Are abductions carried out by lone or multiple offenders? Are witnesses generally present? Who reports the crime to law enforcement agencies? Is violence a frequent aspect of parental child-stealing? Do the offender and victim disappear after the crime, or is communication established with the custodial parent?

Understanding the situational elements of child-snatching can be aided by knowledge of the precipitating factors of the crime. For parental child-stealing, this requires the analysis of legal conditions and the form of custodial arrangement. What type of custody awards are endemic to parental child-stealing? Is joint custody common in such cases? Are conflicting custody orders common in parental child-stealing offenses? Such data will prove essential to a detailed analysis of the nature of parental child-stealing.

Methodology of the Study

To date there has been no study dealing with the patterns of parental child-stealing. Therefore, in selecting a population of parental child-stealing offenses, the major concern was to obtain as much data pertaining to the crime as possible. After extensive conversations with law enforcement personnel, attorneys, and policy makers and a review of the literature, it was determined that local district attorney files would contain the most abundant information concerning parental child-stealing.

Once authorization for the study was secured, retrieving the cases for analysis required some unusually delicate negotiations and procedures. In order to implement sampling procedures it was necessary to acquire a list of all Penal Code secs. 278 and 278.5 cases[7] by the Prosecutors Management Information System (PROMIS),[8] from the district attorney's administrative unit. Although these offense categories include the abduction of a child by extended family members such as an aunt or grandparent, the cases selected for study are limited only to instances of a child abducted or detained by a parent in violation of a custody decree.

The cases under study include cases filed and rejected for prosecution by the district attorney's office between July 1, 1977 and June 30, 1978. This time period encompasses parental child-stealing cases filed with the district attorney during the initial year of California's new law prohibiting such activity.

The PROMIS list of parental child-stealing offenses provided individual case numbers for each case. For logistical purposes, it was necessary to organize the cases identified through PROMIS by specific branch offices. Branch offices contained as many as sixty-eight cases in the Central office, and as few as nine cases in the Compton office. The author reviewed all case files utilized in this study during a five-month period.

Negotiation with branch offices for review of files was generally troublefree.[9] Branch offices were extremely cooperative in all but three instances. In the Compton, Long Beach, and Torrance offices, the author was denied access to individual case files. These three offices accounted for forty-two parental child-stealing cases identified through PROMIS. In each instance the confidentiality of criminal justice information statutes were interpreted by the supervising attorney as excluding the author. Specifically, Penal Code sec. 11076 was noted as forbidding the author access to these files. The statute reads: "Criminal offender record information shall be disseminated, whether directly or through an intermediary, only to such agencies as are, or may subsequently be, authorized access to such records by statute."[10]

Extensive consultation with district attorney personnel followed. The author decided to abandon retrieval of the cases held by these three branch offices for two reasons. First, because the research was not departmentally mandated or staffed and therefore "unofficial," the author was requested to overlook those cases in question or seek alternate data sources. And secondly, in reviewing the ninety-one cases that comprise this study, the district attorney's office was extremely gracious and helpful.

Arrangements were made with each branch office for the review of records. A data collection form was designed after an initial examination of six case files and lengthy discussions with staff members from the Central records unit.[11] For each file reviewed, data was transferred onto the data form.

The official case records were dichotomous in data content. When the offender and victim were located, a wealth of information was available. For these cases, the official records usually included: initial crime report, follow-up investigation report, district attorney reviews, marriage dissolution and child custody orders, probation reports, correspondence from offenders or custodial parents, and final determination information. But when the parties were at large, information within the official case records was sparse. Records for many of the cases rejected for prosecution were limited to no more than the crime report, and for some of these cases even that was unavailable. Other cases were destroyed or misplaced. The author was able to secure crime reports on a few of these missing cases that were rejected for prosecution by cross-checks that yielded police report numbers and by the assistance of personal acquaintances in law enforcement. Once all cases were examined a check for disposition and sentence was made through PROMIS.

The examination of parental child-stealing in this study is made on the basis of data contained in district attorney records only. Cases of parental child-stealing were analyzed regardless of whether the offender was known to police, apprehended, or prosecuted.

Use of Official Records

Perhaps in no area of social science more than in the study of deviance and crime is the balance between credibility and rigorous methodology more difficult to achieve. Investigations in these areas are often governed by flexibility and compromise. Flexibility may be necessary for studying specific behavior when it is required that work be done within the prescribed limits of the situation without sensitizing the actors, and compromise may be required when access to information is limited, and the application of basic tenets of research impractical. A crucial aspect of work in the field of criminology is that of deciding what methods of research are applicable to the phenomenon under study.

There is almost universal dissatisfaction with the accuracy of official reports of crime.[12] Most people are left in a quandary as to how much official records understate or overstate the problem. The major dissatisfaction with official records is traceable to the role of law enforcement officers. The discretion to determine if a crime has occurred and what information will be collected to make that decision are normally police functions.[13] As one national study concluded: "The police must make important judgments about what conduct is in fact criminal; about the allocation of scarce resources; and about the gravity of each individual incident and the proper steps that should be taken."[14] Official indexes of crime must be viewed cautiously because they are based only on crimes which have been detected and acted upon by law enforcement personnel.

The difficulty in accurately gauging crime from official records is governed by the invisibility of the act and the victim's unwillingnes to report it. The victim's hesitancy in reporting[15] and an officer's reluctance in acting upon a parental child-stealing event are often based upon the feeling that the law is beyond the scope of "domestic disputes."[16] As Kitsuse and Cicourel state, "Rates of deviant behavior are produced by the actions taken by persons in the social system which define, classify and record certain behaviors as deviant."[17] Clearly, the enforcement officer's discretion to decide if a crime has been committed,[18] and the unwillingness of victims to report crimes, can seriously distort official accounts of criminal activity.

In dealing with police statistics, we must not forget the inherent pitfalls contained in their use. The complainant may refuse to report the crime. The futility of inaction, especially in child stealing cases, would increase the nonreporting of offenses. The victim may change his or her story, thereby making the police skeptical about whether or not it is the truth. The police can act indifferent to or dismiss a case in which there is a slight suspicion of false accusation. The race,[19] the age, and the previous criminal record of the offender[20] may also influence police decisions, especially when there is no specific or available custody decree. Also, police personnel who record and investigate parental child-stealing complaints carry with them biases toward certain kinds of domestic lifestyles, for example, those in which there are race and age differences between the parties involved or those involving extended family members or cohabitation relationships. All of these may be viewed skeptically by police.[21]

It is a widespread belief that police employ idiosyncratic procedures when dealing with different crimes and offenders. The sex offender may be more vigorously pursued, or blacks may be arrested with less evidence than is needed to arrest a white person. Police are also reluctant to intervene in family matters which involve volatile emotions and complex relations. These factors and others may influence the reliability of parental child-stealing data from police utilized in the present study. Still, early exponents of police data as a base for research realized the value of a register of actual offenses committed without reference to subsequent detention or adjudication.[22]

A detailed examination of parental child-stealing demands as much information, direct or indirect, as possible to understand the complex and delicate underpinnings of this crime. It was, therefore, advantageous to use district attorney records. Among the reasons influencing the use of prosecutor records, rather than, for instance, only police or prison records were: (1) they offer the opportunity to follow cases over a lengthy period of time through the justice system; (2) for each case in the study, a police crime report was available; many cases also included probation reports, court documents, dissolution of marriage and custody decrees, and correspondence; (3) although it was acknowledged that attrition increases as one selects a study point further into the justice system, it is believed that inclusion of rejected cases would minimize the effect of system mortality; and (4) of all the possible sources of data regarding parental child-stealing, district attorney records are the single most complete source of data.

Since child-stealing offenses can be prosecuted as either felonies or misdemeanors at the district attorney's discretion, the more serious felony cases are generally handled by that office, while the city attorney prosecutes solely misdemeanor child-stealing offenses.[23]

City attorney cases usually entail less serious but more protracted domestic disharmonies. If one acknowledges Bonger's caution that "the amount of crime actually punished . . . may not be an affixed or unveering ratio to the amount of crime committed,"[24] the fact remains that district attorney records provide the most complete data to study this unique crime.

Prosecutorial crime data can be biased by a number of factors.[25] Because the law allows an optional felony-misdemeanor charge, cases in which the location of the child is unknown or a prior child-theft has occurred are charged as a felony. This is necessary since, for practical purposes, extradition is remote in misdemeanor offenses. A custodial parent may also inflate the seriousness of the offense to use the district attorney's office as a threat to bring about compliance to a custody order or induce the child's return. The custodial parent may also reconsider prosecution of an ex-spouse and withdraw the complaint upon acquisition of the child. Many parental child-stealing cases remain unsolved and their status unclear because the whereabouts of the offender and child are unknown or the confusion between inter-jurisdictional agencies precludes a final determination.

Child-stealing cases forwarded to the district attorney can be rejected for prosecution for a number of reasons. A case is rejected if the child is over sixteen years of age or above the age of discretion. Rejection as a felony charge also occurs if it is known that the child remains within California, and the case will be referred to the city attorney for misdemeanor prosecution. And parental child-stealing will not be prosecuted if the child was abducted from an abusive or blatantly unstable family setting.

In addition to the above limitations of prosecutorial records, one special problem was identified concerning parental child-stealing cases. Official records depict only one view of an enormously complex picture often involving a web of relationships and actions. It should be recognized that at times an offender may rationalize very persuasive reasons for abducting the child. He or she may be aware of an imminent change of residence by the guardian, thus, precluding visitation privileges. The court-ordered visitation rights may have been denied or episodically granted. The abduction may be a futile effort to remove the child from a dilapidated homelife. In many cases of parental child-stealing, the offender is not without merit, morally and legally. The custodial parent may have induced or contributed to the culminating act of abduction.

The interests of each agency were evident in the case records. Police reports were the most encompassing and afforded the best description of the transgressions. District attorney records were a strict application of police information to prosecution-charging guidelines. Variation in the quality of records from office to office was negligible. Probation reports, which were generally rare, attempted to assess the offender's character and lifestyle. It should be noted that probation reports rely heavily upon data supplied by the offender. Prior court decrees specified clear direction for the care of the child. For cases unresolved, usually pending location of the offender, data became noticeably attenuated.

Conviction statistics were rejected as the basis for this study because they may reflect the cultural norms held by judges or juries,[26] public opinion of the period about that specific crime,[27] or the differential administration of justice in regard to certain groups.[28] Social class and race influence the ability of the plaintiff to be adequately defended, for instance.

Parental child-stealing cases processed by the district attorney still provide the most valid and comprehensive data we now have to describe the nature of parental child-stealing. They afford a more credible and inclusive understanding of this crime than probation or prison statistics. At present, there is no realistic alternative to district attorney records.

However, the use of official records warrants more general discussion. In considering the broader aspects of information contained in official records, we may identify two major drawbacks: the definition of terms and the methods of data collection.[29] Frequently definitions used for official categories do not coincide with those used in scientific research. Second, varying methods of data collection may distort and alter the true nature of official statistics. Questions raised include: Were the data collecting methods adequate? Were the informants able and willing to give information to the original collector of information?

Definitions

A number of terms are basic to this investigation of the nature of parental child-stealing. Some of these terms have been used in different ways in prior research, and some are employed in different senses in one or another's jurisdiction's laws on child-stealing. To be sure that the terms are consistently applied the present study will define these terms in the following manner:

Child—A son or daughter below eighteen years of age.

Custodial parent—The parent specified in a custody award responsible for the child's control, care, and maintenance.

Custody decree (or custody)—A determination as to the control, care, and maintenance of a child by an award of the court.

Parent—The lawful father or mother of a child by blood relations.

Parental child-stealing—A parent abducting or detaining a child from the custodial parent in violation of a custody order.

Stealing (abduction, snatching, or theft are used synonymously)—To take or detain a child from its parent as specified by a custody order.

Victim—The abducted child.

Research with official records demands imagination to perceive their usefulness and a willingness to follow an unconventional line of data collection.[30] The content limitations of official records, however, may not be as great as the social scientist bound by orthodoxy believes. The Chinese proverb still seems valid: "The palest ink is clearer than the best memory."

Notes

1. Marvin E. Wolfgang, *Patterns in Criminal Homicide* (Philadelphia: University of Pennsylvania Press, 1958).

2. Menachem Amir, *Patterns in Forcible Rape* (Chicago: University of Chicago Press, 1971).

3. John Conklin, *Robbery and the Criminal Justice System* (Philadelphia: J.B. Lippincott Co., 1972).

4. Albert Morris, *Homicide: An Approach to the Problem of Crime* (Boston: Boston University Press, 1954), p. 4.

5. Special appreciation is due Martin Oghigian and Robert Altman of the Los Angeles County District Attorney's Office.

6. See, for instance, Anna Demeter, *Legal Kidnaping* (Boston: Beacon Press, 1977); Dave Smith, "Kidnaping With Impunity," *Los Angeles Times*, 19 April 1976; Kay Bartlett, "Child Snatching—A Family Affair," *Sacramento Bee*, 19 September 1976; Joy Horowitz, "The Law Has Few Answers For Child Stealing Cases," *Los Angeles Herald Examiner*, 21 March 1977; Dave Smith, "Father Outruns Law in Child Custody Case,"

Los Angeles Times, 3 August 1977; Suzanne Ramos, "When Parents Steal Their Own Children," *New York Times*, 15 November 1979, sec. c, p. 1; Lindsy Van Gelder, "Beyond Custody: When Parents Steal Their Own Children," *Ms.*, May 1978, p. 52; Scott Winokur, "The Child Stealers," *San Francisco Examiner*, 5 October 1980; Judy Foreman, "Kidnapped! Parental Child-Snatching A World Problem," *Boston Globe*, 16 March 1980; and Robert Gore, "Child Stealing on Increase Across U.S.," *Los Angeles Times* (West Side Edition), 25 May 1980.

7. Cal., Penal Code, secs. 278-278.5 (West Supp. 1977).

8. See Los Angeles County District Attorney's Office, *Prosecutor's Management Information System: PROMIS User's Manual*, Los Angeles, 1977; and Sidney Broustein and William Hamilton, "Analysis of the Criminal Justice System with the Prosecutors Management Information System (PROMIS)," in *Qualitative Tools for Criminal Justice Planning*, ed. Leonard Oberlander (Washington, D.C.: U.S. Government Printing Office, 1975), p. 91.

9. Data was collected from the following branch offices: Central, Norwalk, Pasadena, Pomona, Santa Monica, and Van Nuys.

10. Cal., Penal Code, sec. 11076.

11. See Appendix A.

12. Donald Cressey, "The State of Criminal Statistics," *National Probation and Parole Journal* 2 (July 1957):230-241; and Michael J. Hindelang, 'The Uniform Crime Reports Revisited," *Journal of Criminal Justice* 2 (Spring 1974):1-17.

13. James Wilson, *Varities of Police Behavior* (Cambridge: Harvard University Press, 1968), pp. 83-110.

14. President's Commission on Law Enforcement and Administration of Justice," *Task Force Report: The Police* (Washington, D.C.: U.S. Government Printing Office, 1967), p. 14.

15. Anne Schneider, Janie Burcart, and L.A. Wilson, "The Role of Attitudes in the Decision to Report Crime to the Police," in *Criminal Justice and the victim*, ed. William McDonald (Beverly Hills: Sage Publications, 1976), pp. 89-113.

16. Raymond Parnas, "Police Discretion and Diversion of Incidents of Intra-Family Violence," *Law and Contemporary Problems* 36 (Autumn 1971):539.

17. John Kitsuse and Aaron Cicourel, "A Note on the Use of Official Statistics," *Social Problems* 11 (Fall 1963):131-139.

18. Jerome Skolnick, *Justice Without Trial: Law Enforcement in Democratic Society* (New York: John Wiley & Sons, 1966).

19. Gilbert Geis, "Statistics Concerning Race and Crime," *Crime and Delinquency* 2 (April 1965):142-150.

20. William Westley, "Violence and the Police," *American Journal of Sociology* 59 (July 1953):34-41.

21. Raymond Parnas, "The Police Response to the Domestic Disturbance," *Wisconsin Law Review* (1967):1-914.

22. Thorsten Sellin, "The Significance of Records of Crime," *Law Quarterly Review* 67 (October 1951):489-504.

23. Cal., Penal Code, sec. 17b-4. Even if the district attorney files felony charges, they can be reduced to a misdemeanor at the preliminary hearing.

24. William Bonger, *Race and Crime*, trans. M. Hordyke (Montclair: Patterson-Smith Publishing, 1943), p. 34.

25. Frank Miller, *Prosecution: The Decision to Charge A Suspect With A Crime* (Boston: Little, Brown & Co., 1969).

26. See Arthur Vanderbilt, *Judges and Jurors: Their Functions, Qualifications and Selection* (Boston: Boston University Press, 1956); and Willard Gaylin, *Partial Justice: A Study of Bias in Sentencing* (New York: Visage Press, 1974).

27. U.S. Department of Justice, *Public Opinion About Crime: The Attitudes of Victims and Nonvictims in Selected Cities* (Washington, D.C.: U.S. Government Printing Office, 1977).

28. Michael J. Hindelang, "Equality Under the Law," *Journal of Criminal Law, Criminology & Police Science* 60 (September 1969):306-313.

29. Claire Selltiz, Marie Jahoda, Morton Deutsch, and Stewart Cook, *Research Methods in Social Relations*, revised ed. (New York: Holt, Rinehart & Winston, 1959), pp. 322-323.

30. Eugene Webb, Donald Campbell, Richard Schwartz, and Lee Sechrest, *Unobtrusive Measures: Nonreactive Research in the Social Sciences* (Chicago: Rand McNally Co., 1966), pp. 84-87.

2

A Perspective of Family Violence

Lizzie Borden took an ax and gave her father 40 whacks.
When the job was neatly done, she gave her mother 41.
                    Rhyme popular after murder trial,
                    Fall River, Massachusetts, June, 1893

America is quickly learning that the family is hardly an oasis of serenity and comfort. Violence between family members has become increasingly common. The limited data available indicates that intrafamily violence is increasing in both frequency and seriousness. Recently, criminologists have taken up the study of family violence.[1] These studies concern instances in which a victim has incurred serious physical or emotional harm and comes to the attention of public agencies such as the police, hospitals, or prosecutors.[2] What is known of the extent and nature of family violence may be the "tip of the iceberg." Existing research about crimes between family members has been limited generally to such areas as wife beating, homicide, child abuse, and incest or child molesting.

The following section reviews the general nature of family violence. As Strauss has cautioned: "I don't think we understand violence in the family. . . . The home is where violence primarily occurs."[3] The following data cannot imply any direct association between various types of violence or parental child-stealing. It is presented, however, to sketch a perspective of the family structure as a unit considerably more crime prone than previously conceived. Parental child-stealing can be viewed as one type of crime within the increasingly violent domestic environment.

Homicide between Family Members

Intrafamily homicide has a long history, starting with the Biblical story of Cain slaying Abel.[4] Although relatively rare, murder has received considerably more public attention than less violent yet more common forms of family violence. More murders are committed by family members within the family than by any other type of person. The FBI reports that in 1978 there were 3,911 homicides between family members—20 percent of all homicides.[5] The 1977 figure for homicides between family members was 3,633, which comprised 19 percent of homicides for that year.[6] In 1976, the number of intrafamily homicides was 5,071, or 27 percent,[7] and in 1975 there were 4,101 instances, or 22 percent,[8] in which the victims were related to the offender. These national figures report 2,359 spouse murders in 1975, which is 11 percent[9] of the total homicides that year. The wife was the victim in 52 percent and the husband was the victim in 48 percent of the 1975 spouse murders.[10]

The most thorough study of homicide to date, Wolfgang's analysis of 588 criminal homicides in Philadelphia between 1948-52, found that nearly 28 percent of the cases involved offenders and victims of the same family.[11] The study noted that of the 136 victims who had familial relations with their slayers, 100 were husbands or wives, 9 sons, 8 daughters, 3 mothers, 3 brothers, 2 fathers, 1 sister, and 10 others.[12] The research found that when women killed men, they always used weapons to overcome the male's greater strength, but beating was the method men used to kill women in 23 percent of the cases in which women were victims.[13] Women were more likely than men to be killed where they lived—68 percent were killed in the home, whereas 46 percent of all men murdered were killed in the home. Also, 55 percent of those women killed in the home—as compared to 35 percent of the men—were killed in a home they shared with their assailants.[14] Wives killed by their husbands constituted 41 percent of all women who were killed, although husbands killed by their wives made up only 11 percent of all men who were killed.[15]

A 1960 study of 200 women imprisoned in California found that 63 percent of these women had killed their husbands or lovers.[16] A study by Palmer in 1969 found that murderers are the targets of tremendously greater amounts of violence as children than their siblings.[17] Such children were nearly beaten to death as youths, and as adults they often did beat someone to death.

Domestic Assault

> *A woman, a spaniel, and a walnut tree;*
> *The more they're beaten, the better they be.*
> Old English Proverb, 1732

Assaults by husbands against their wives, or "wife beatings," have been supported throughout history. The "rule of thumb" is rooted in English Common Law and grants a husband the right to beat his wife with a stick "no thicker than his thumb."[18] Domestic assault is generally considered to include forms of violent behavior between people who live together, which is done with the intention of inflicting bodily harm.[19] Such spouse abuse is often deliberate and severe and occurs repeatedly.

Data assessing the extent of domestic assault is very limited. Many women do not register complaints with authorities.[20] Police, when responding to a domestic assault, may not file a report, or, if they do, wife beating would be included in the broader category of assault and battery.[21] Data from hospital emergency rooms is also limited because medical doctors are reluctant to probe the cause of injuries that suggest domestic assault. As Rounsaville observes:

> The victims of wife-battering have received little focused attention from medical and mental health professionals. Battered women present to medical facilities vague complaints, traumatic injuries, or trouble with the children. Most often the busy practitioner deals with the presenting complaint at face value and makes few inquiries about its origin.[22]

Estimates suggest that spousal assault is a growing and serious problem. Perhaps the most encompassing study of intrafamilial violence is by Gelles.[23] From extensive interviews he found that forty-four of the eighty families studied reported physical violence between spouses.[24] Family violence most frequently occurs in the kitchen, while the bedroom and living room are the next most likely scenes of violence.[25] Most violence, 37 percent of the cases, occurred in the evening between eight and eleven thirty; the early evening hours between five and eight o'clock accounted for 22 percent of the cases.[26] Weekends accounted for 69 percent of the violence,[27] and in no instance was someone other than the immediate family members present during the violence.[28]

Husbands were the more violent party; they reported hitting their wives at least once in 47 percent of the cases, while 32 percent of the wives struck their husbands.[29]

A survey conducted for the National Commission of the Cause and Prevention of Violence, investigating what types of violence people would approve of, found that one out of every four men and one out of every six women approve of slapping a wife under certain circumstances. Of a wife slapping her husband, 26 percent of the men and 19 percent of the women approved.[30] One of the most accurate measures of spousal assault to date comes from a 1977 nationwide survey of couples living together which estimated that one or the other partner in over 1.7 million couples had faced a spouse wielding a gun or knife, over 2 million had been beaten by their spouses, and another 2.5 million had engaged in high-risk-of-injury violence.[31]

The Kansas City Police Department found that it had responded to disturbance calls at the addresses of homicide victims or suspects at least once in the two years before the homicide in 90 percent of the cases, and five or more times in the two years before the homicide in 50 percent of the cases. They had responded once to disturbance calls at the homes of victims or suspects in 85 percent of the aggravated assault cases, and five or more times to disturbance calls in 50 percent of these cases during two years before the aggravated assault.[32] Of the cases studied, 42 percent involved physical force, but when the participants were either married or divorced, the incidence of force rose to 54 percent. When the participants were common law spouses, relatives, strangers, or acquaintances, however, physical force occurred about only 31 percent of the time.[33]

In 1974, Boston police responded to 11,081 family disturbance calls, most of which involved physical violence. At the end of the first quarter of 1975, they had received 5,589 such calls—half the previous year's figure in one quarter of the time.[34] Further, Boston City Hospital reported that approximately 70 percent of the assault victims received in its emergency room are known to be women who have been attacked in their homes, usually by a husband or a lover.[35] The Citizens' Complaint Center in the District of Columbia receives between 7,500 and 10,000 complaints of marital violence each year.[36] Approximately 75 percent of the complainants are women. In Detroit, 4,900 wife-abuse complaints were filed in 1972.[37] In New York, 14,167 wife-abuse complaints were processed statewide by the Family Court in 1972-73.[38] A St. Louis study notes that husbands or wives are the victims in 11 percent of the city's aggravated assaults. It also found that in acts of homicide a wife attacks her husband more than a husband attacks her, but the reverse is true in aggravated assault.[39]

Studies of marital dissatisfaction among persons seeking divorce indicate that marital disharmony is often expressed in violence. In a 1969 study of 150 persons seeking divorce, the research found that violence between spouses was of sufficient intensity to be central to the initiation of the divorce. For persons married between thirteen and thirty-seven years, violence was mentioned by 64 percent of the respondents, while 36 percent of the persons married between one to five years reported violence. Most reports of marital violence—84 percent—came from women. O'Brien was able to classify 48 percent of the violence as behavior occurring chronically throughout the marriage.[40]

In another study of 600 couples with at least one child under fourteen years of age, who were divorce applicants, Levinger found that 37 percent of the wives as compared to only 3 percent of the husbands complained that their spouses hurt them physically. Verbal abuse was reported to be a major complaint by 24 percent of the wives and 7 percent of the husbands.[41]

The above data clearly indicates the seriousness of domestic assault as a growing problem. Because of the many limitations in gathering accurate information, the full extent of wife beating remains unknown.[42]

Child Abuse

Child abuse is the physical abuse of children by their parents. The National Child Abuse Center reports that in 1978 nearly six hundred thousand children in America were victims of abuse or neglect.[43] Zelba projects that between two hundred thousand and two hundred fifty thousand children in the United States need protective services, and that thirty thousand to thirty-seven thousand may be badly hurt by their parents each year.[44] Gil conservatively estimates that six thousand children each year are severely beaten by their parents.[45] A clear picture of the true extent of child abuse, however, is limited because of problems with defining which actions constitute child abuse.[46] Should child abuse encompass neglect, physical injury, sexual abuse, or a combination of acts?[47] Also, underreporting is believed to be extensive since child abuse is usually discovered only after serious physical injury has been inflicted.

Child abuse, especially by persons caring for the children, appears to be an extension of physical force during the process of child rearing. Gelles found that children were struck by their parents at least once in 96 percent of the cases he examined and that violence toward the children occurred on a monthly basis for 45 percent of the families.[48] Such abuse is not limited solely to physical harm, but can also include emotional trauma.[49] A child's witnessing of violence between parents can induce fear, guilt, or shock. Child abuse carries the potential to increase future violence within the family. The effects of child abuse are cumulative. A large majority of delinquent adolescents indicate that they were abused as children.[50] And abused children often grow up to become abusive spouses: one study reports that nearly 38 percent of battered wives reported physically abusing their children, and 54 percent of these women claimed that their husbands also physically harmed their children.[51] As Pizzey states from her long experience in providing services for victims of domestic violence in England:

> A man who batters is a child who was battered that nobody helped. If we look at the history of these men, they are either beaten children or actually watched it . . . so the violence goes on from one generation to the next. It becomes the norm.[52]

Child abuse, therefore, may serve as the catalyst for future and more severe forms of family violence.

Police and Family Violence

The police are the first line of response for victims of family violence. Yet police are reluctant to respond to domestic disturbance calls and rarely deem an arrest necessary.[53] This may be due, in part to the fact that family violence is a dangerous area for law enforcement. Husband-wife or parent-child calls are the single most risky situations for police. The FBI reports that of police officers killed in the line of duty, 9 percent in 1978,[54] 24 percent in 1977,[55] 18 percent in 1976,[56] and 16 percent in 1975, died trying to break up a family disturbance.[57] Crisis intervention training, in fact, is usually geared to protecting the police.

The reluctance of police to assist in family violence calls is also supported by the fact that many forces prefer a nonarrest policy. Good police work for family disputes has been acknowledged to be the avoidance of arresting participants.[58] The International Association of Chiefs of Police has adopted the view that "in dealing with family disputes, the power of arrest should be exercised as a last resort."[59] Police, therefore, strive to settle the immediate situation. What is practiced to resolve intrafamily disputes is mediation, adjustment, or referrals.[60] The police give low priority to family violence calls because: (1) the victim is believed to be tied economically and socially to the offender; (2) the police know that the District Attorney will rarely prosecute such cases; and (3) the victim is likely to withdraw the complaint.

In a sample of 283 calls over a two-month period in Vancouver, British Columbia, it was found that a car was dispatched nearly 54 percent of the time for man-woman fights. In only 10 percent of the cases did these calls receive priority attention. If the caller mentioned violence, weapons, and alcohol, the probability went up to 67 percent, and if children were involved, then it went up to 73 percent. The decision to dispatch a police car was not based on the availability of personnel or vehicles, because the dispatch rate did not fluctuate with the time of day or day of week. The arrest rate for these cases was about 7 percent.[61]

In a 1967 study of the Chicago Police Department's response to family violence, Parnas observed that there was no official policy or practice in responding to such calls—in spite of the fact that domestic dispute calls comprised 50 percent of all calls for assistance.[62] The study found a consistent pattern of nonarrest, adjustment, and referral based upon police officer experience. Parnas calls this action the "support function":

> In exercising the support function—the use of alternatives other than arrest in aid of both disputants—it is uncertain whether this police response is a recognition of the underlying value of preserving the private, personal, intimate, or family integrity of the disputants, or whether their response results from an awareness of the practical difficulties (time lost for numerous court appearances in which complainant withdraws) inherent in either a full enforcement or no response approach to domestic disturbance. . . . Practical and value-oriented approaches to dealing with domestic disturbances lead in the direction of adjustment rather than arrest.[63]

Parnas also found that the Chicago police dispatchers failed to obtain sufficient information to adequately set a priority level or to inform the responding officer of danger from weapons. As soon as police determined that an intrafamily disturbance was the reason for the call, no questions were asked, and the incident was classified a "domestic disturbance." Parnas concluded that such a response was inadequate to provide meaningful assistance to family members and resulted in many police officer injuries and deaths.[64]

The reluctance to intervene in family violence leads police to define as nonviolent all family disputes, unless blood is drawn or injuries are clearly visible. Such attitudes reinforce violence, and offenders learn that lesser forms of violence are tolerated by the system.

Notes

1. See Suzanne K. Steinmetz and Murray A. Straus, eds., *Violence in the Family* (New York: Dodd, Mead & Co., 1975).

2. John Martin, ed., *Violence and the Family* (New York: John Wiley & Sons, 1978).

3. Mary Kuhn, "There's No Place Like Home for Beatings," *Washington Star*, 11 November 1975.

4. Gen. 4:1-15.

5. U.S., Department of Justice, *Uniform Crime Reports-1978* (Washington, D.C.: U.S. Government Printing Office, 1979), p. 8.

6. U.S., Department of Justice, *Uniform Crime Reports-1977* (Washington, D.C.: U.S. Government Printing Office, 1978), p. 9.

7. U.S., Department of Justice, *Uniform Crime Reports-1976* (Washington, D.C.: U.S. Government Printing Office, 1977), p. 10.

8. U.S., Department of Justice, *Uniform Crime Reports-1975* (Washington, D.C.: U.S. Government Printing Office, 1976), p. 18.

9. Ibid., pp. 18-19.

10. Ibid., p. 9.

11. Marvin E. Wolfgang, *Patterns in Criminal Homicide*, p. 207.

12. Ibid., p. 212.

13. Ibid., pp. 85-87 and 215-216.

14. Ibid., p. 123.

15. Ibid., p. 213.

16. David Ward, Maurice Jackson, and Renee Ward, "Crimes of Violence by Women," in *Crimes of Violence*, National Commission on the Cause and Prevention of Violence (Washington, D.C.: U.S. Government Printing Office, 1969), pp. 843-909.

17. Stuart Palmer, *The Psychology of Murder* (New York: Thomas Y. Crowell Co., 1960), pp. 76-80.

18. Marjory Fields, "Wife Beating: Facts and Figures," in *Notes from the Women's Rights Project*, volume 2 (New York: American Civil Liberties Union, 1977), p. 2.

19. See *Victimology: An International Journal* 2 (1977-78), special issue on spouse abuse.

20. Erin Pizzey, *Scream Quietly or the Neighbours Will Hear* (Baltimore: Penguin Books, 1974).

21. Darrel Stephens, "Domestic Assault: The Police Response," in *Battered Women*, ed. Maria Roy (New York: Van Nostrand Co., 1977), pp. 164-172.

22. Bruce Rounsaville, "Battered Wives: Barriers to Identification and Treatment," *American Journal of Orthopsychiatry* 48 (1978):487.

23. Richard J. Gelles, *The Violent Home: A Study of Physical Aggression Between Husbands and Wives* (Beverly Hills: Sage Publications, 1972).

24. Ibid., p. 48.

25. Ibid., p. 95

26. Ibid., p. 100.

27. Ibid., p. 104.

28. Ibid., p. 107.

29. Ibid., p. 51.

30. Rodney Stark and James McEvoy, "Middle Class Violence," *Psychology Today*, November 1970, pp. 52-65.

31. Murray A. Straus, Richard J. Gelles, and Suzanne K. Steinmetz, *Behind Closed Doors: Violence in the American Family* (New York: Doubleday, 1980), p. 33.

32. G. Marie Wilt, James Bannon, and Ronald K. Breedlove, eds., *Domestic Violence and the Police: Studies in Detroit and Kansas City* (Washington, D.C.: Police Foundation, 1977), pp. 22-23.

33. Ibid., p. 27.

34. Laura White, "Women Organize to Protect Selves From Husbands," *Boston Herald American*, 22 June 1975.

35. Betsy Warrior, "Battered Lives," *Houseworkers Handbook* (Spring 1975):25, cited in *Battered Wives* by Del Martin (San Francisco: Glide Publications, 1976), p. 255.

36. Lois Yankowski, "Battered Women: A Study of the Situation in the District of Columbia," (Washington, D.C., Womens Legal Defense Fund, 1975), pp. 2-3.

37. James Bannon, "Law Enforcement Problems with Intra-Family Violence" (Speech delivered at the American Bar Association Conference, Toronto, Canada, 12 April 1975).

38. J. Barden, "Wife Beaters: Few of Them Ever Appear Before a Court of Law," *New York Times*, 21 October 1974, p. 38.

39. David Pittman and William Handy, "Patterns in Criminal Aggravated Assault," *Journal of Criminal Law, Criminology & Police Science* 55 (September 1963):462-470.

40. John O'Brien, "Violence in Divorce Prone Families," *Journal of Marriage and the Family* 33 (November 1971):692-698.

41. George Levinger, "Sources of Marital Dissatisfaction Among Applicants for Divorce," *American Journal of Orthopsychiatry* 36 (October 1966):804-806.

42. See Del Martin, *Battered Wives*; and Donna Moore, ed., *Battered Women* (Beverly Hills: Sage Publications, 1979).

43. American Humane Association, *Highlights of 1978 National Reporting Data* (Colorado: American Humane Association, May 1979), p. 1.

44. Serapio Zelba, "Battered Children," *Trans-Action* (July-August 1971):58-61.

45. David Gil, "Violence Against Children," *Journal of Marriage and the Family* 33 (November 1971):637-648.

46. See David Finkelhor, *Sexually Abused Children* (New York: Free Press, 1979), pp. 53-72.

47. See *Victimology: An International Journal* 2 (Summer 1977), special issue on child abuse and neglect.

48. Gelles, *The Violent Home*, p. 53.

49. See Harold Martin and C. Henry Kempe, *The Abused Child* (Cambridge, Mass.: Ballinger Publishing Co., 1976); and Richard Bourne and Eli Newberger, eds., *Critical Perspectives on Child Abuse* (Lexington: D.C. Heath & Co., 1979).

50. Ray Hefler and C. Henry Kempe, eds., *Child Abuse and Neglect* (Cambridge, Mass.: Ballinger Publishing Co., 1976), p. xviii.

51. J. Gayford, "Wife Beating: A Preliminary Survey of 100 Cases," *British Medical Journal* 11 (1975):194-197; and similar findings were noted in Larry Silver, Christina Dubin, and Reginald Lourie, "Does Violence Breed Violence? Contributions from A Study of the Child Abuse Syndrome," *American Journal of Psychiatry* 126 (September 1969):404-407.

52. As quoted in Judith Weinraub, "The Battered Wives of England: A Place to Heal Their Wounds," *New York Times*, 29 November 1975, p. 17.

53. In general, "domestic disturbance" or "family dispute" are terms used by police departments to describe a wide range of incidents, often minor, involving members of the same household—whether or not they are related by blood or marriage. These terms would, for example, cover verbal disagreements between husband and wife, assaults between a man and a woman living together, arguments between parent and child, and threats and actual instances of physical assault between household members.

54. U.S. Department of Justice, *Uniform Crime Reports-1978*, p. 307.

55. U.S. Department of Justice, *Uniform Crime Reports-1977*, p. 292.

56. U.S. Department of Justice, *Uniform Crime Reports-1976*, p. 288.

57. U.S. Department of Justice, *Uniform Crime Reports-1975*, p. 225.

58. Morton Bard and Harriet Connolly, "The Police and Family Violence: Policy and Practice," in *Battered Women: Issues of Public Policy*, U.S. Commission on Civil Rights (Washington, D.C.: U.S. Government Printing Office, 1978), p. 307.

59. International Association of Police Chiefs, *Training Key No. 16: Handling Disturbance Calls* (Gaithersberg: International Association of Police Chiefs, 1965), p. 3.

60. Morton Bard and Joseph Zacker, *The Police and Interpersonal Conflict: Third Party Intervention Approaches*, monograph (Washington, D.C.: The Police Foundation, 1976).

61. Donald Dutton, "Domestic Disturbance Intervention by Police" (Paper presented at the Symposium on Family Violence, Vancouver, British Columbia, 1977).

62. Raymond Parnas, "The Police Response to the Domestic Disturbance," *Wisconsin Law Review* (1967):914.

63. Ibid., p. 955.

64. Ibid., p. 922.

3

The Extent of Parental Child-Stealing

There is a scarcity of accurate statistical data on the frequency of parental child-stealing in America. Official figures are usually incomplete, are combined with multiple offense categories, or are nonexistent. The FBI does not compile information about parental child-stealing on a national basis. Arrest register data from the California Bureau of Criminal Statistics found 136 adults arrested during 1977, 208 arrested in 1978, and 213 arrested in 1979 for violations of Penal Code sec. 278.[1] The Los Angeles County District Attorney reports that between January 1975 and April 1979, 400 cases of child-stealing were screened, of which 240 were rejected for prosecution.[2] The Los Angeles County Sheriff's Department reported 60 child-stealing cases in 1977, with that figure increasing to 86 in 1978, and 65 cases in 1979.[3] The Los Angeles Police Department reported 163 cases of parental child-stealing for 1977, while the 1978 figure increased to 190 cases, and 179 instances were reported in 1979.[4]

There is strong reason to suspect that the official picture of child-stealing suffers from substantial underreporting. Unofficial estimates suggest that there are twenty-five thousand to one hundred thousand outright child-thefts per year in America.[5] When the retention of children after visitation is included, the taking of children from custodial parents may reach four hundred thousand cases annually.[6] And indications are that child-snatchings are increasing rapidly in the United States, now reaching perhaps as many as twenty-five thousand cases each year.[7]

Restealing of Children

The increasing frequency of child-thefts coupled with the tedious and ineffective legal process of settling custody disputes has given rise to a new industry of sorts—"custody vigilantes." For fees between three hundred dollars to ten thousand dollars, custodial parents are being aided by a growing cadre of specialists who recover children by restealing. Since the well publicized *Mellon* case in 1976,[8] restealing by professionals, or parental agents as they are known under the law, has become more frequent.[9]

For example, Gene Austin is such an agent who works almost exclusively for fathers. Austin has a thousand requests per year and boasts over two hundred snatches, with only one conviction. In a recent divorce case, during which the mother abducted the child to Florida after a Missouri decree awarding the child to the father, Austin recounts the snatching at the mother's apartment:

> We staked it out until she was out in the back yard with Benjamin. Then we moved in to get him. We went up to her and tried to grab the child and she started hollering for her boyfriend, who came charging out of the house with a baseball bat. We had to wrestle her to the ground and give her a light Macing. I started to neutralize the boyfriend, but I saw he was going to hit a tree with the bat. Sure enough, he did—and he broke the bat, too.[10]

Using rental cars and sleeping over in "safe houses" provided by sympathizers, Austin delivered the child to his father three days later. And other self-styled custody missionaries have claimed to have reacquired up to one thousand children. The majority of these snatchers incorporate such assignments into private detective operations.[11]

Divorce Trends Relating to Parental Child-Stealing

The full extent of child-stealing can only be crudely estimated because law enforcement agency data is incomplete, but the potential for possible child-thefts can be better gauged. Divorce is rapidly increasing in America. In 1978, Americans divorced 1,122,000 times.[12] The rate of divorce has increased steadily, and the 1960 rate of 2.2 divorces per one hundred thousand population increased in 1970 to 3.5, and in 1978, the rate reached 5.1.[13] The number of children involved in divorce has nearly tripled between 1960 and 1976, increasing from 463,000 to 1,117,000 children.[14] With the number of child-stealing cases estimated at between twenty-five thousand to one hundred thousand, this amounts to about one child-theft for every 22 divorces. Such a rapid increase in the divorce rate signals the potential for an epidemic of parental child-thefts. Recognizing that not every divorce contains the social chemistry which spawns child-stealing, one may observe that the potential for victimization has, neverthelss, greatly increased.

There also has been a rapid increase in the number of one-parent families between 1960 and 1978. By 1978 the data indicates that 19 percent of families with children were being maintained by one parent—17 percent by mothers and 2 percent by fathers.[15] This increase of one-parent families rose from the 1960 figures of 8.5 percent—7.4 percent by mothers and 1.1 percent by fathers.[16] Today, almost two million children live in one-parent families.

Currently, more fathers have become more desirous of obtaining custody of their children. Single fatherhood increased 32 percent between 1970 and 1978, with nearly one million American children under the age of eighteen living with their male parents.[17] Backed by the proliferation of fathers' rights organizations,[18] men are refusing to become discarded artifacts churned from the divorce process whose responsibility ends with financial support.[19]

The difficulty for both children and adults to function in a society becoming increasingly characterized by ruptured and strained family relations has been noted by Fain:

> There are at lease three million children of divorce under eighteen years of age in the U.S. today, and the divorce courts are adding about 300,000 more children to this group each year. Perhaps 50 percent of the divorce cases which go through the nation's courts have minor children involved, averaging about two children per couple. The manner in which the courts deal with these victims of domestic catastrophe has an impact, directly or indirectly, on substantial portions of our people. It presents a challenge to the stability of our social institutions and is assuming threatening significance.[20]

These divorce and family data suggest that child-stealing holds the possibility of affecting a large segment of Americans. All indications suggest that child-stealing occurs substantially more than is recorded and that as domestic relations become increasingly unstable, divorce and child custody decrees will be more frequently challenged, which should also increase the frequency of child-thefts.

Effects of Divorce

Divorce is a legal, emotional, and social process through which the marital relationship is dissolved. Its participants are susceptible to a variety of damaging factors. As Bogue notes:

> Few events in the life-cycle require more extensive changes in activities, responsibilities and living habits (or cause greater alterations in attitudes, reranking of values and alterations of outlook on life) than does a change from one marital status to another.[21]

Divorce may produce episodes of deep sadness, loneliness, fear, anxiety, or euphoria, among others.[22] The impact of divorce is so great that research has linked it with, among other things, poor health,[23] depression,[24] mental illness,[25] and a low level of life satisfaction.[26]

Of special importance to the study of parental child-stealing is the extent of bitterness or malice between spouses created by divorce.[27] Because continued communication between spouses generally is necessary for the care of the child, the relationship does not end at divorce. Divorce signals a new phase of the now ruptured relationship. The extremely volatile arena of post-divorce can generate hostility and vindictiveness that affects such areas as child custody, visitation, or financial support. Hostility in this phase of the relationship can surface in plans for revenge or retaliation. The parenting of children, therefore, becomes a convenient vehicle for the expression of such malice.[28]

At the time of separation, child custody is likely to be the major area of conflict.[29] The division of real property usually is easily accomplished, but the care and possession of the child is fraught with emotions and controversy. The Bible tells us that in trying to determine the true parent of a child in question, Solomon understood that the desire for custody can lead to deceit and vindictiveness and determined the true parent only after threatening to divide the child in two.[30]

Once custody has been determined, conflict over the care of children does not end. Each spouse is vulnerable to the other because of the shared contact with the child.[31] Each may fear that the child is being turned against him or that the courts have created an impenetrable wall around his children. Organizing visitation programs with the custodial parent establishes that the child is now in that parent's control and that the visiting parent is a fringe family member or "outsider." A custodial parent may set obstacles or strict guidelines in allowing visitation, such as permitting visitation only in the presence of the custodial parent or offering visitation at blatantly inconvenient times. The noncustodial parent may buy excessive gifts or stress negative qualities of the other parent. Berating the ex-spouse during visitation may be effective in undermining that parent's authority. Such behavior encourages a parent to desire total control over the child, and the created hostility may ultimately give rise to the illegal abduction of children.

Notes

1. Correspondence with Dennis Bartholomew, California Bureau of Criminal Statistics, 4 March 1980. No data is available for Cal., Penal Code, sec. 278.5.

2. Correspondence with Martin Oghigian, Los Angeles County District Attorney's Office, 14 September 1979.

3. Correspondence with Murle Hess, Los Angeles County Sheriff's Department, 2 April 1980.

4. Correspondence with J.D. Smith, Los Angeles Police Department, 8 April 1980.

5. See Dave Smith, "Kidnaping With Impunity," p. 1; Kay Bartlett, "Child Snatching—A Family Affair," p. 1; Joy Horowitz, "The Law Has

Few Answers for Child Stealing Cases," p. 8; Dave Smith, "Father Outruns Law in Child Custody Case," p. 1; and Suzanne Ramos, "When Parents Steal Their Own Children," p. 1.

6. "Abduction of Own Child Could Result in Felony," *Los Angeles Daily Journal*, 3 March 1976.

7. Meredith McCoy, *Parental Kidnaping: Issues Brief No. IB 77117* (Washington, D.C.: Congressional Research Service, 1978).

8. Fred Ferretti, "2 Mellon Children Abducted Here in Custody Battle," *New York Times*, 20 March 1976, p. 1.

9. John Huey, "To Man Whose Job Is Child Snatching, End Justifies Means," *Wall Street Journal*, 24 March 1976, p. 1.

10. Ibid., p. 1.

11. "Kidnapping: A Family Affair," *Newsweek*, 18 October 1976, p. 24.

12. U.S., Department of Commerce, Bureau of the Census, *Current Population Reports: Divorce, Child Custody and Child Support*, 84, June 1979, p. 1.

13. Ibid., p. 1.

14. Ibid., p. 8.

15. Ibid., p. 1.

16. Ibid., p. 9.

17. U.S., Department of Commerce, Bureau of the Census, *Current Population Reports: Marital Status and Living Arrangements March 1978* 388, May 1979, p. 6.

18. Among such organizations are: Association for Parents Rights (Sacramento, California), Childrens Rights Inc. (Washington, D.C.), Fathers Demanding Equal Justice (Los Angeles, California), and United Parents of Absconded Parents (Cuba, New York).

19. See Robert Hanley, "Fathers Group to Fight Custody Decision," *New York Times*, 7 March 1977, p. 57; and Daniel Molinoff, "Life With Father," *New York Times*, 22 March 1977 (magazine), p. 12.

20. Harry Fain, "1963 Proceedings," Section of Family Law, American Bar Association, in *Readings in Law and Psychiatry*, eds. Richard Allen, Elyce Ferster, and Jesse Rubin (Baltimore: Johns Hopkins University Press, 1968), p. 316.

21. Donald Bogue, *The Population of the United States* (Glencoe: Free Press, 1949), p. 212.

22. Jack Westman and David Cline, "Divorce Is a Family Affair," *Family Law Quarterly* 5 (March 1971):1-10.

23. Robert Chester, "Health and Marital Breakdown: Some Implications for Doctors," *Journal of Psychosomatic Research* 17 (November 1973):317-321.

24. C. William Briscoe and James Smith, "Depression and Marital Turmoil," *Archives of General Psychiatry* 29 (December 1973):811-817.

25. Monica Blumenthal, "Mental Health Among the Divorced," *Archives of General Psychology* 16 (May 1967):603-608.

26. Robert Weiss, "The Emotional Impact of Marital Separation," *Journal of Social Issues* 32 (1976):135-145.

27. See Ann Demeter, *Legal Kidnaping*, pp. 21-41; and also *Alternative Lifestyles* 2 (November 1979), special issue on ending intimate relationships.

28. Joseph Goldstein, Anna Freud, and Albert Solnit, *Beyond the Best Interests of the Child* (New York: Free Press, 1973).

29. See Robert Weiss, *Marital Separation* (New York: Basic Books, 1975).

30. Kings 1:16-28.

31. Mel Roman and William Haddad, *The Disposable Parent: The Case for Joint Custody* (New York: Holt, Rinehart & Winston, 1978).

4 The Law and Parental Child-Stealing

Parental authority over one's child has been a fundamental aspect of our society. This authority has recently become complicated with the demise of many two-parent families. This shift in marriage patterns, combined with the failure of legal measures to adequately define child custody rights, has created enormous legal difficulties.

The problems of child custody and support when the parents are separated or divorced exists even when the parents are responsible, cooperative, and make an effort to resolve their differences amicably. The bounds of parental authority are exceeded, however, when a parent abducts his child against the will of the child or the other parent or guardian. This legal chaos has given rise to what Justice Jackson has described as the law of the jungle "where possession . . . is not merely nine points of the law but all of them."[1] This recent phenomenon of child-stealing has created intricate legal problems which span the civil, criminal, and welfare codes of American jurisprudence.

This chapter will focus on the omissions, conflicts, and deficiencies of the legal sanctions which not only permit but also appear to encourage what has become a national problem. In addition, recent legislation within California to clarify the law relating to parental child-stealing will be analyzed.

The Federal Kidnaping Act

Legal sanctions concerning kidnaping in America have traditionally addressed "a wide and ill-defined range of behavior."[2] The legal basis for kidnaping is the taking or detention of a person against his or her will or without lawful authority. Historically, the label "kidnaping" has been applied to a variety of unlawful takings with intentions including: defilement, prostitution, ransom, robbery, skyjacking, and the general transportation of a person against his or her will.

The creation of the federal noncapital kidnaping law, expedited by the *Lindbergh* case,[3] was signed by President Hoover on June 22, 1932 and became a capital crime in 1934.[4] This federal kidnaping act was initially applicable only to interstate kidnaping for ransom, reward, or "other unlawful purposes."[5] The federal statutes, one might expect, would provide adequate statutory provisions against child-stealing. During committee debate, however, concern was voiced that the code would lead to the prosecution of parents who take their children across state lines against a custody decree or to avoid jurisdiction.[6] In response, the federal statutes specifically exclude "kidnaping" of a minor by his parent, as the present federal regulations state: "of otherwise, except, in the case of a minor, by a parent thereof."[7] It is therefore not a federal crime for a parent to abduct his child even in violation of a valid custody decree.

The Fugitive Felon Act[8] makes it a felony for anyone to travel interstate to avoid prosecution for a felony. But this statute is ineffective because the Department of Justice will not utilize the act in child-stealing cases unless an additional felony is committed or if "the circumstances indicate that either the physical or moral welfare of the child will be impaired."[9] The U.S. attorney is hesitant to enter child-stealing cases because they are deemed domestic matters outside of the purview of the federal kidnaping regulations. The Federal Bureau of Investigation has been similarly uncooperative and has ignored recent appeals for aid in child-stealing cases on the grounds that no federal law has been violated. Therefore, the resources of the FBI cannot be implemented to locate offending parents.

Extradition is rarely invoked because of the domestic character of childstealing and the common practice of prosecutors to file misdemeanor, not felony charges. Also, the fact of provincialism—a desire to protect the local parent and his or her view of the interests of the child—frequently blocks extradition efforts. Even in those rare instances when an extradition request is honored, there is no provision for the return of the child.

Jurisdiction for Child Custody

Kidnaping laws protect both parental rights and children's personal liberty against infringement from third parties. Parental status, however, has been used as an effective defense against kidnaping charges. The posture of custody rights and child protection has become compromised because of the incongruities within the law and procedural variations between jurisdictions. Statutes are conflicting and disorganized: the welfare codes address the interests of the child, the civil laws govern the changing domestic status of the parents, and kidnaping is the concern of criminal codes.

Child-stealing has evolved into a self-help method of settling custody disputes. Immunity of parents from child-stealing has been created because parental custody privileges have superseded the child's right to justice. With "equal" custody rights in California, parents "have joint custody of the child . . . and neither has rights superior to those of the other."[10] During the pendency of dissolution of a marriage, present law provides that the court may make a custody order.[11] There is no requirement, however, that such an order be made. Thus, it is actually legal for a parent to take and conceal the child or leave the state, even after a petition for dissolution or an action seeking custody has been filed.

This seize-and-run approach, especially in interstate cases, has become even more attractive to parents because safety is further guaranteed by procedural conflict between courts.[12] An absconding parent is frequently granted a custody hearing in the destination state, even though he has defied a custody decree in the original state.[13] Usually the justification for granting a new custody hearing is said to be the state's concern for the welfare of the child. Bodenheimer suggests a less altruistic reason:

> The practice that custody decisions must always remain open to change for the child's benefit, is in fact often employed in the interests, not of the child, but of his feuding parents or relatives.[14]

The granting of a new custody hearing in another jurisdiction leads to unendng changes in the original custody decree. The sense of power and conflict between judges granting new custody jurisdictions has been distinctly described by Justice Fairchild as "due to a tendency of any individual to think that in a situation demanding the wisdom of Solomon he can come closer than anyone else."[15]

The inconsistencies of custody jurisdiction decrees have been created by court infighting. Bodenheimer has identified three factors which give rise to the various jurisdictions granting new custody hearings. First, the second judge may disagree with or mistrust the prior custody judgment. This attitude seems understandable given the fact that custody is determined on the vague notion of the best interests of the child. Without objective standards as to the specific content of "best interests," this is open to broad judicial discretion. Second, there may be a tendency of courts to be a little more receptive to the parent who is a local resident, present with the child, and professes to assume full responsibility. Competition between courts may cause a judge to disregard the original judgment of other courts. What must be recognized is that in addition to a parental power struggle for possession of the child, there may be a judicial power struggle. Third, the court, parents, and lawyers often become confused in the emotionalism inherent in the custody dilemma.[16]

Equal treatment of both parents has become a physical impossibility. Ultimately parents must face the harsh reality of divorce and realize that children, unlike property, cannot be fractioned. This is made increasingly evident by the impact of recent efforts to use "joint custody" to achieve parental equality.[17]

The interstate recognition of judicial determinations is mandated by the full-faith-and-credit clause of the Constitution.[18] This provision has been administratively limited to "final" decrees. Decree orders relating to child custody, visitation, and support are nonfinal in the sense that they are invariably open to modification pending a change of circumstance. If the first jurisdiction may modify, it is therefore possible for subsequent jurisdictions to invoke changes outside the purview of the full-faith-and-credit clause.[19] Although most states are apt to give prior decrees strong consideration, it is Florida and New York that have shown the least concern for upholding prior custody decisions. Justice Frankfurter, supporting the need for flexible custody decrees, has stated:

> Because the child's welfare is the controlling guide in custody determination, a custody decree is of an essentially transitory nature. The passage of even a relatively short period of time may work great changes, although difficult of ascertainment, in the needs of a developing child. Subtle, almost imperceptible, changes in the fitness and adaptability of custodians to provide for such needs may develop with corresponding rapidity. A court that is called upon to determine whom and under what circumstances custody of an infant will be granted cannot, if it is to perform its function responsibly, be bound by a prior decree of another court.[20]

This practice has created an unending process of jurisdictional encroachment between courts at the direct expense of the child's home stability.

Frequently, a parent will attempt to secure a custody decree or modify another state's decree by taking the child to another state. This search for a custody hearing in a new court jurisdiction is called "forum shopping." With full knowledge that a parent who now seeks a custody decree has brought the child into court by violation or some other misconduct, courts have frequently reopened child custody decrees. These courts are acting against the principle of "clean hands."[21] This principle requires a denial of relief to an individual who is himself guilty of inequitable conduct in reference to the matter in controversy.[22] The court will not even listen to such a petitioner because his conduct is in itself reprehensible. Such support of parental misconduct further encourages interstate parental child-stealing.

A common justification of the failure to apply the clean hands principle is the belief that it is wrong to punish a child for misconduct by parents. Misconduct by parents must be superseded by the court's concern for the welfare of the child. In 1889 the Pennsylvania Supreme Court recognized "instinctive parental behavior"[23] as a rationale for overlooking clean hands. And the Court reaffirmed its disregard for clean hands in 1974 by stating:

> In this type of case where parents attempt to outwit each other in the possession and custody of their children, we will not place much weight

on the frailties of human nature, nor subordinate more important factors, especially since these regrettable acts on the part of the parents are in the past.[24]

Such sympathetic treatment granted abducting parents is further exemplified in a California decision.[25] A child in the legal custody of her mother residing in California accompanied her father for a two-week vacation to his home in Texas. The father refused to return the child and initiated proceedings for a custody change in Texas and was awarded custody by the Texas Court. The Texas decree specified the mother's visitation rights solely in the state of Texas. The mother then kidnaped her daughter and returned to California. She was charged with kidnaping in Texas, but California refused extradition. The California Court granted custody to the mother, citing the best interests of the child and that if the father were given custody, the mother would be unable to visit the child without risking liability to the kidnaping offense. This rewarding of parents for interstate child stealing by courts which fail to invoke the clean hands principle also encourages forum shopping.

States use one of three bases for original jurisdiction in determining custody disputes: domicile of the child, residence of the child, or personal jurisdiction over both parents.[26] Domicile, the place with which one has the most settled connection and considers to be "home,"[27] is the strictest standard because it requires the greatest degree of permanence. In California, a child cannot choose a domicile until eighteen years of age, so when parents separate, the children assume the domicile of the parent with whom they live or with whom the court places them.

The majority of states accept residence, a physical presence within the state, as an adequate basis for jurisdiction. Willingness to accept such a meager basis is found in the concept of "parens patriae."[28] Once a child is present within the state, the state has an interest in his welfare. Courts have, however, refrained from any direct exercise of parens patriae in child-stealing cases. These special protection decrees in the form of emergency jurisdiction control are regularly utilized to stop child abuse or to insure the safety of battered children. Parens patriae is reserved, generally, for application when the life or health of the child is seriously threatened. But courts have held that the exercise of jurisdiction in cases of a minor's welfare is an unavoidable duty stemming from the parens patriae doctrine. Judge Cardoza has written:

> The jurisdiction of a state to regulate the custody of infants found within its territory does not depend upon the domicile of the parents. It has its origin in the protection that is due to the incompetent or helpless. For this, the residence of the child suffices, though the domicile be elsewhere.[29]

The granting of domicile on mere physical presence, coupled with the court's inclination to favor the local petitioner, is yet another invitation for forum shopping. The failure of courts to practice clean hands and give full-faith-and-credit to prior jurisdiction custody decrees punishes the law-abiding parent and rewards the law-violating parent with possession of the child. Regardless of good intent and compassion, such judicial practice creates a legal process which does not serve the best interests of the child, the parents, or justice.

In sum, child stealing by a parent is induced by the incongruities within the legal process because of: (1) the general ineffectiveness of the statutes available; (2) the failure of states to give full-faith-and-credit to prior decrees; (3) the sporadic and limited practice of the clean hands doctrine; and (4) the favoring of the local petitioner in custody decrees.

Because the federal kidnaping act excludes parents, and in some cases their agents, expansion of federal law to cover child-stealing and, therefore, to subject parents to criminal prosecution has been proposed.[30] Federal legislation has offered to include child-stealing by parents under the federal kidnaping act and impose imprisonment up to one year and a one thousand dollar fine, or both, when a person is convicted of interstate child-stealing. This would give clear authority to the Federal Bureau of Investigation to investigate such cases and facilitate the location of stolen children. This proposal has met strong opposition by federal law enforcement agencies.[31] They exhibit no desire to intervene into a traditionally domestic controversy within states. Bodenheimer questions the effect of federal criminal sanctions against child-stealing:

> . . . The criminal law is not equipped to make the necessary distinctions between flagrant violators of the law and persons whom one might call "meritorious offenders," that is, parents who take the law into their own hands as long as other states refuse, under traditional doctrine, to enforce their custody rights under a prior decree. In addition, incalculable damage may be done to a child by the arrest and incarceration of the parent with whom he is living.[32]

The Uniform Child Custody Jurisdiction Act

Recognizing an ever increasing national problem because of conflicting inter-jurisdictional custody laws, the National Conference of Commissioners of Uniform State Laws drafted the Uniform Child Custody Jurisdiction Act[33] which was approved by the American Bar Association in 1968. The basic goal of the act is that jurisdiction for custody decisions be limited to the state which has maximum access to the facts to avoid what Justice Traynor has described as "interminable and vexatious litigation."[34] The act's goal to reduce jurisdictional conflict was stated by the Commissioners on Uniform State Laws as:

> Underlying the entire Act is the idea that to avoid the jurisdictional conflicts and confusions which have done serious harm to innumerable children, the court in one state must assume major responsibility to determine who is to have custody of a particular child; that this court must reach out for the help of courts in other states in order to arrive at a fully informed judgment which transcends state lines and considers all claimants, residents and nonresidents, on an equal basis and from the standpoint of the welfare of the child. If this can be achieved, it will be less important "which" court exercises jurisdiction but that courts of the several states involved act in partnership to bring about the best possible solution for a child's future.[35]

To date, the act has been adopted by forty-three states and became effective as California law in 1974 as Civil Code secs. 5150-5174.[36] The entire scope of the act, however, has not been fully utilized in California.

The first point of the act is that one court in the country assumes full responsibility for custody of a particular child. For this purpose, a court is selected which has access to as much relevant information about the child and family in the state as possible. The proper forum to determine custody of the child is the "homestate." This is defined in the act as "the state in which the child immediately preceding the time involved lived with his parents, a parent, or a person acting as parent for at least six months."[37] If the child is less than six months of age, the homestate is the state the child lived in from birth with any of the above stated. Periods of temporary absence, caused by travel for example, are counted as part of the six-month period. Other states are to defer to and cooperate with the homestate while it retains jurisdiction under the act.

In addition to the homestate basis for jurisdiction, the act has a general provision which applies when it is in the best interests of the child. The court retains the jurisdiction to act as parens patriae. This is for emergency situations in which the child may, for example, be abandoned.[38] If the family has moved frequently and there is no state in which the child has lived six months, the "significant connections" test shall determine jurisdiction.[39] Under this clause, jurisdiction exists only if it is in the best interests of the child for the court to assume jurisdiction. The child's interests, however, may not coincide with those of the feuding relatives.

Because of this continuing jurisdiction under the homestate, the act remains applicable even if the child has been removed from the state. The act does not demand physical presence of the child for a custody decree, although it is desirable.[40] The act's main intention is to avoid conflicting jurisdiction at initial custody proceedings.

To reduce the casual modification of out-of-state decrees, the act incorporates the full-faith-and-credit doctrine[41] and extends it to uphold not only the prior decree but also the continuing jurisdiction of the rendering court.[42] This means that a petition for modification is to be addressed to the original court.

Once deference to the original court is given by the second court, as a rule, there should be a marked lessening of interstate child-stealing. When a new court is approached with a petition for modification, it would be sent back to the original court.

The act's objective to avoid relitigation can only be achieved if all the persons claiming custody of the child can be satisfied in the same proceeding. The act is designed to bring all known contestants into the custody proceeding. To accomplish this, the act uses a number of steps:

1. Parties are to inform the court of other persons claiming legal custody or having physical custody of the child.
2. The court is required to join these individuals as parties to the litigation.
3. Strict requirements for due process, notification, and opportunity to be heard are prescribed.
4. Once proper jurisdiction is used, a decree binds all parties specified as noted in California Civil Code sec. 5161.
5. A decree is recognized and enforced in other states.[43]

The act further directs that other essential evidence which might be out of state be channeled into the first or "custody state." To insure the most enlightened and lasting decree, the act strives to coordinate and assist the efforts of the original court by upholding the full-faith-and-credit doctrine. To this end, the act addresses the warning of Professor Bodenheimer, who served as reporter on the Uniform Child Custody Jurisdiction Act for the Commissioners of Uniform State Laws:

> Anyone who seriously attempts to find a solution for the unhappy spectacle of interstate custody battles will probably conclude that in addition to a uniform law which stresses interstate judicial assistance and cooperation, there is a definite need for the development of new judicial attitudes toward interstate custody cases. No one state is in a position, singlehandedly and in isolation, to determine a child's future when a portion of the essential evidence inevitably is elsewhere across state boundaries.[44]

An out-of-state custody decree which is recognized under the act is automatically enforceable in another state by filing a copy of the decree with the clerk of the appropriate court.[45] The decree becomes a local decree and enforceable by contempt proceedings or other means.[46] Excluding emergency situations, the power to enforce does not include the power to modify. Visitation provisions are enforceable in the same manner as primary rights to custody.

The act is not without its limitations: *It is effective only in states that have also adopted the act*; there is no check provision should the homestate render an erroneous custody decree; the act protects such misjudgments and contains no basis for modifying such decisions. Jurisdiction to grant a divorce and custody decree may not be conterminous. Should the divorce forum not be the child's homestate, custody rights would have to be determined in subsequent litigation, and some states may choose to utilize only selected aspects of the act such as California, which generally applies sec. 5158 of the act in child custody cases. The act lacks provision for obtaining physical custody of the child to prevent removal from another state. Yet the effectiveness will ultimately depend on the number of states adopting the act and the good faith with which its provisions for cooperation and communication are implemented.

California Law through 1976

Prior to July 1, 1977, California law provided that the father and mother of a legitimate unmarried minor child were "equally" entitled to its "custody, services and earnings,"[47] and Civil Code sec. 198 held that the father and husband had no rights superior to those of the wife and mother in regard to the "care, custody, education and control" of the child while they lived apart from each other.[48] Because parents had equal rights, neither parent was in violation of the law, civil or criminal, by taking and concealing the child in the absence of a court order awarding custody to a particular parent.

In addition, while Civil Code secs. 4600 and 4603 provided for a court adjudication of custody whether or not a divorce decree had been filed, there was no requirement that such a decree be made.[49] Under past California law, in the absence of a judicial order granting custody to one parent, it was not a crime for one parent to detain or conceal the child. Child-stealing circumvented the legal statutes of California because it was possible for a parent to take the child, or leave the state or country, even after a petition for dissolution of marriage had been filed, without violating a court order. California Civil Code statutes were, therefore, clearly inadequate to curb child-stealing by parents.

California Penal Codes have previously defined parental child-stealing as a form of child abduction. The codes ranged in seriousness from either a twenty-year prison sentence to a misdemeanor offense with a maximum punishment of a five hundred dollar fine or one year in country jail, or both. The first California statute, Penal Code Sec. 278, stated

> Every person who maliciously, forcibly, or frauduently takes or entices away any minor child with intent to detain or conceal such child from its

parent, guardian, or other person having the lawful charge of such child, is
punishable by imprisonment in the state prison not exceeding twenty years.[50]

The effectiveness of this code was limited for a number of reasons. First, kidnaping charges were usually dismissed because of the inability to establish
"malicious" taking. Proof of malice required a showing by specific facts that
the abducting parent intended to annoy or injure another person (usually the
other parent) or do a wrongful act.[51] Even if the prosecution could show
malice, the offending parent had an opportunity to show that he or she was
acting in the best interests of the child, and, if so, held an adequate defense
against child abduction.

A second problem with sec. 278 was that the prosecution had to show that
the offending parent had intended to detain or conceal the child *at the time of
the taking*. It was not a crime for a natural parent merely to detain or conceal
the child, and if the prosecution was incapable of proving a felony, extradition was lost. Thus, the statute was ineffective because the initial taking by a
parent usually was neither forcible nor fraudulent.

The second California statute attempting to deal with parental child-
stealing was Penal Code sec. 279.[52] This code prescribed as a misdemeanor
the detention, concealment or removal of a child in violation of a custody
order. The law stipulates that:

> Every person who has actual physical control of a child for a limited period
> of time in the exercise of the right to visit with, or to be visited by, such child,
> or the right to limited custody of such child, pursuant to an order, judgment
> or decree of any court, which order, judgment or decree grants custody of
> such child to another, and who, without good cause and with intent to detain
> or conceal such child, keeps said child in this state after the expiration of such
> period without the consent of the person or persons entitled to custody of
> such child, violates this section.[53]

The ability of this statute to restrain child-snatching was limited because
the prosecution had to establish that the conduct occurred in California and
that the parent acted "without good cause." Once again, in the absence of a
charged felony, extradition was practically impossible.

California Law from 1977

As a result of Assembly Concurrent Report 236 in 1974,[54] which documented
the limitations and omissions of the California laws, Assemblyman Michael
Antonovich introduced, on September 5, 1975, legislation designed to reform
existing law and make child-abduction in violation of a custody decree a
criminal offense.[55] The legislation, Assembly Bill 2549,[56] was signed into law

October 1, 1977, and became operative July 1, 1977. By transferring child-stealing from the civil to the criminal jurisdiction, the new California law is a strong and direct response to this increasingly common problem.

Generally, Assembly Bill 2549 toughens sanctions and clarifies certain legal procedures dealing with child stealing. Sec. 278 and 279 of the Penal Code were modified and reenacted as the present 278 and 278.5[57]

Penal Code sec. 278, child abduction, now applies to "person(s) not having a right of custody."[58] It is no longer necessary to establish that the offending parent intended to take the child *at the time of the taking*. It is sufficient to show only that the child was detained or concealed. This makes the law more prosecutable. Malice for a criminal act must still be proven of anyone who "takes, entices away, detains or conceals any minor child from a parent or guardian. . . ."[59] The section is applicable mainly to friends, relatives, or strangers other than parents who take or conceal a child from an individual with the right of custody. This section is punishable as a felony and stipulates imprisonment in state prison for a maximum of four years, a fine of not more than ten thousand dollars, or both, or one year in county jail and a one thousand dollar fine, or both.[60]

Penal Code sec. 278.5, which replaced Penal Code sec. 279, directly relates to parents who act against a custody decree and take a child from the legal custodian. This section also enforces a parent's visitation rights and makes it a crime for a parent to refuse visitation privileges incorporated in a custody decree. The statute reads:

[Violation of custody decree; punishment; return; expenses]
(a) Every person who in violation of a custody decree takes, retains after the expiration of a visitation period, or conceals the child from his legal custodian, and every person who has custody of a child pursuant to an order, judgment or decree of any court which grants another person rights to custody or visitation of such child, and who detains or conceals such child with the intent to deprive the other person of such right to custody or visitation shall be punished by imprisonment in the state prison for a period of not more than one year and one day or by imprisonment in a county jail for a period of not more than one year, a fine of not more than one thousand dollars ($1,000), or both.
(b) A child who has been detained or conceals in violation of subdivision (a) shall be returned to the person having lawful charge of the child. Any expenses incurred in returning the child shall be reimbursed as provided in Section 4605 of the Civil Code. Such costs shall be assessed any defendant convicted of a violation of this section.[61]

No longer is the criminal act required to take place in California. If, for example, a child leaves the custodial parent in California for visitation with the second parent in another state and that parent refuses to return the child to the custodial parent in California at the expiration of the mandated visitation period, Penal Code sec. 278.5 is still applicable. If the custodial parent is a resident of California, a violation of Penal Code sec. 278.5 can be shown. Also, since "good cause" is no longer a defense for parental child-stealing, the offending parent's motives are irrelevant.[62]

Penal Code sec. 278.5 is an alternate felony-misdemeanor offense which allows the prosecution to charge a felony if desired. The charging of a felony makes available the possibility of extradition to properly adjudicate the case.

The new legislation also requires a petition for temporary custody to be included with a filing for dissolution of marriage pending a final custody determination.[63] In addition, courts may issue arrest warrants to insure the appearance of offending parties at hearings.[64] Courts will also notify persons having rightful custody of a child who may be in another state, as well as the out-of-state district attorney, after refusing jurisdiction because of wrongdoing on the part of the parent who has physical custody of the child.[65] Also, courts now have authority to order persons in California lacking legal custody to return a child to persons having rightful custody, or the court may assume temporary custody of the child unlawfully removed from California at the offending parent's expense.[66]

One of the primary difficulties in child-stealing is the problem of locating the abducted child and returning him to the appropriate jurisdiction for custody adjudication. Assembly Bill 2549 instructs the district attorney in California to "take all actions necessary to locate such party and the child and to procure compliance with the order to appear with the child for purposes of adjudication of custody."[67] In addition, the cooperation of all state, county and local agencies in the location of abducting parents and stolen children is mandated.[68]

Secondly, the Central Registry of Absent Parents in the California Department of Justice Parent Locator Service, previously limited to finding parents for enforcement of child support obligations, will be expanded to provide local agencies assistance in child-abduction cases.[69] It has access to records of all public agencies. The new legislation also authorizes the attorney general to utilize the federal parent locator service of the Department of Health, Education, and Welfare when necessary.

Assembly Bill 2549 addresses many major problems of California law relating to child-stealing. The legislation, however, fails to curb certain specific types of child custody problems. For instance, parents A and B initiate dissolution of marriage proceedings. Prior to being served formal court dissolution and temporary custody decrees, parent A takes the child and flees California. Parents who take their child and leave California prior to a custody decree are acting within their parental rights and are not acting illegally. A second type of child-stealing not addressed by Assembly Bill 2549 is the case of A and B living together with no marriage contract and producing a child. If either father or mother absconds with the child, no custody decree has been violated. Such actions regarding child-stealing are exempted by Assembly Bill 2549.[70]

This California legislation is a significant effort toward clarifying numerous legal discrepancies and oversights which have prompted parents to utilize child-stealing as an extralegal method of securing their children. Although the new California laws fails to categorically address every possibility of child-stealing by parents, they can be viewed as a major contribution to the reduction of this serious and growing problem.[71]

Notes

1. Justice Jackson dissenting in *May* v. *Anderson*, 345 U.S. (1953): 528-529.

2. "A Rationale of the Law of Kidnapping," *Columbia Law Review* 53 (April 1953):540.

3. "Lindbergh Baby Kidnapped From Home of Parents on Farm Near Princeton; Taken From His Bed; Wide Search On," *New York Times*, 2 March 1932, p. 1.

4. U.S., Act of May 18, 1934, chap. 301, 48 Stat. 781-782.

5. See Ernest Alix, *Ransom Kidnapping in America 1874-1974* (Carbondale: Southern Illinois University Press, 1978).

6. See U.S., Congress, Committee on the Judiciary, *Hearings on H.R. 5657*, 72d Cong., 1st sess., 1932, p. 5; and "The Problem of Parental Kidnapping," *Wyoming Law Journal* 10 (Spring 1965):225.

7. 18 USC, sec. 1201.

8. Ibid., sec. 1073.

9. U.S., Congress, Subcommittee on Crime, *Hearings on H.R. 4191 and H.R. 8722*, 93d Cong., 2d sess., 1974, p. 38.

10. Regarding custody during marriage see Cal., Civ. Code, sec. 197 (West).

11. Cal, Civ. Code, secs. 4600 and 4603.

12. Jane Lewis, "Legalized Kidnapping of Children by Their Parents," *Dickinson Law Review* 80 (Winter 1976):205-237.

13. See Albert Ehrenzweig, "The Interstate Child and Uniform Legislation: A Plea for Extra-Litigious Proceedings," *Michigan Law Review* 64 (November 1965):1-12; and Leonard Ratner, "Legislative Resolution of the Interstate Child Custody Problem: A Reply to Professor Currie and a Proposed Uniform Act," *Southern California Law Review* 38 (Spring 1965): 183-205.

14. Brigitte Bodenheimer, "The Uniform Child Custody Jurisdiction Act," *Family Law Quarterly* 3 (March 1969):304.

15. Justice Fairchild of the Wisconsin Supreme Court (Speech delivered at the Conference of Chief Justices, St. Louis, 8 August 1961).

16. Bodenheimer, "The International Kidnapping of Children: The United States Approach," *Family Law Quarterly* 11 (Spring 1977):83-100.

17. See Mel Roman and William Haddad, *The Disposable Parent: The Case for Joint Custody*; and Charlotte Baum, "The Best of Both Parents," *New York Times*, 31 October 1976, p. 44 (magazine); and Miriam Galper, *Co-Parenting—Sharing Your Child Equally* (Philadelphia: Running Press, 1978). See also, Alice Abarbanel, "Sharing Parenting After Separation and Divorce: A Study of Joint Custody;" *American Journal of Orthopsychiatry* 49 (April 1979):320-329. Regarding California's joint custody law enacted in January, 1980, see Cal., Civ. Code, sec. 4600.5.

18. U.S., *Constitution*, art. 4, sec. 1.

19. Homer Clark, *The Law of Domestic Relations in the United States* (St. Paul: West Publishing Co., 1968), p. 325.

20. Justice Frankfurter in *Kovacs* v. *Brewer*, 356 U.S. 612 (1958).

21. Albert Ehrenzweig, *A Treatise on the Conflict of Law* (St. Paul: West Publishing Co., 1962), p. 293.

22. See Leonard Ratner, "Child Custody in a Federal System," *Michigan Law Review* 62 (March 1964):795-846; Dale Stansbury, "Custody and Maintenance Law Across State Lines," *Law and Contemporary Problems* 10 (Summer 1944):819-831; and Brainerd Currie, "Full Faith and Credit Chiefly to Judgments: A Role for Congress," *Supreme Court Review* 1964 (November 1964):89-121.

23. *Burns* v. *Commonwealth*, 129 Pa. 138, 18 A. 756 (1889).

24. *Spriggs* v. *Carson*, 229 Pa. Super. 9, 17, 323 A.2d. 275 (1975).

25. *In re Walker*, 228 Cal. App. 2d. 217, 39 Cal. Rptr. 243 (1964).

26. Billie Crouch, "The Full Faith and Credit Clause and Its Relation to Custody Decrees," *Alabama Law Review* 11 (Fall 1958):139-158.

27. Clark, *The Law of Domestic Relations*, p. 144.

28. A concept borrowed from English Common Law as the principle of chancery, "parens patriae" entitled the king to act as "parent of his country" in exercising his power of guardianship over the persons and property of minors who were considered wards of the state and as such entitled to special protection.

29. *Finlay* v. *Finlay*, 240 N.Y. 429, 431, 148 N.E. 624 (1925).

30. They include S. 105 and H.R. 1290, 96th Cong., 1st sess., 1979; H.R. 113 and H.R. 4486, 94th Cong., 1st sess., 1975; and H.R. 8722, 93d Cong., 1st sess., 1974.

31. See U.S., Congress, *Hearings on H.R. 4191 and H.R. 8722*, p. 38.

32. Bodenheimer, "International Kidnapping," p. 99.

33. The Uniform Child Custody Jurisdiction Act is included as Appendix B.

34. *Sampsell* v. *Superior Court*, 32 Cal. 2d. 736, 197 P.2d. 739 (1948), is a frequently cited case that sets jurisdiction in California.

35. Prefatory note to the Uniform Child Custody Jurisdiction Act, as drafted by the National Conference of Commissioners on Uniform State Laws, 1968, p. 6.

36. The act has not been adopted by the following states: Massachusetts, Mississippi, New Mexico, Oklahoma, South Carolina, Texas, and West Virginia. Also, the District of Columbia, Puerto Rico, and the U.S. Virgin Islands have not adopted the act.

37. Cal., Civ. Code, sec. 5152(a).

38. Regarding abandonment and neglect of children in California see Cal., Penal Code, sec. 270.

39. Jurisdiction of a court to decide child custody matters under this principle includes: it being the home state of the child, when it is in the best interests of the child, when the child is physically present in the state, or when it is necessary in an emergency to protect the child from mistreatment or abuse.

40. Cal., Civ. Code, sec. 5152(d).

41. Ibid., sec. 5157(1).

42. Ibid., sec. 5157(2-3).

43. Ibid., secs. 5158-5964.

44. Bodenheimer, "The Uniform Jurisdiction Act," pp. 315-316.

45. Cal., Civ. Code, sec. 5156.

46. Civil contempt is used to compel compliance with a court decree rather than to impose punishment. A parent may be subject to a fine and imprisonment when charged with civil contempt, but these impositions must be conditioned upon continuing noncompliance with the decree. Civil contempt is an effective remedy only when the parent remains in the state.

47. Cal., Civ. Code, sec. 197.

48. Ibid., sec. 198.

49. See Cal., Civ. Code, secs. 4600-4603, prior to July 1, 1977.

50. Cal., Penal Code, sec. 278.

51. Malice as used in the statute imports a wish to vex, annoy or injure the person having lawful charge of the child or an intent to do a wrongful act; see Cal., Penal Code, sec. 7(4).

52. Cal., Penal Code, sec. 279.

53. Ibid., sec. 279(a).

54. California, Department of Justice, *Report to the Legislature—ACR 236*, September 1974, Sacramento.

55. This repeals Cal. Civ. Code sec. 198 which gave "equal rights" to parents.

56. Assembly Bill 2549 (Antonovich), California Legislature, 1975-76, Regular Session.

57. Assembly Bill 2549 also affects the following: repeals Cal. Civ. Code sec. 198; amends Cal. Civ. Code secs. 4600, 4603, 5157, 5160, 5169, Welf. & Inst. Code secs. 11478, 11478.5; adds Cal. Civ. Code secs. 4604, 4605.

58. Cal., Penal Code, sec. 278.

59. Ibid., sec. 278(a).

60. Prior to AB 2549 the maximum punishment was twenty years imprisonment.

61. Cal, Penal Code sec. 278.5.

62. Good cause generally means a legal reason concerned with changed circumstances affecting the child's health or safety. Its existence is based mainly in the discretion of the court.

63. Cal., Civ. Code, sec. 4600.1.

64. For cases within California see Cal., Civ. Code, secs. 5160(o) and 5169(3).

65. Cal, Civ. Code, sec. 5157.

66. Ibid., sec. 4605.

67. Ibid., sec. 4604(a).

68. Cal., Welf. & Inst. Code, sec. 11478 (West).

69. Ibid., sec. 11478.5.

70. Many attorneys believe that in such instances an ex parte order, a determination made by the Court upon application of one of the parties without the other individual, is a valuable means of reducing parental child-stealing.

71. Michael Agopian, "Parental Child Stealing: California's Legislative Response," *Canadian Criminology Forum* 3 (Fall 1980):37.

5 Adjudication of Parental Child-Stealing Offenses

Attempting to examine the interactional elements of any crime is, at best, a difficult task. Parental child-stealing involves a particularly complex skein of behavior and events which require a basic and sensitive analysis of available information. This study examines ninety-one cases of child-theft by parents not having the right to custody that were screened for prosecution by the Los Angeles County District Attorney's Office. The examination of parental child-stealing will consider three primary elements: first, the prosecution of parental child-stealing offenses; second, the participants of the offense—offender, custodial parent, and the child abducted or detained; and, third, the activities, drama, and circumstances that unfold prior to and during the course of the crime.

The perspective sketched in this study presents basic frequencies and percentages of characteristics under analysis. It also uses case narratives extracted from the official files which may be the actual crime reports completed by the investigating officer or records from the prosecuting attorney. The case reports appear verbatim from the official record and are altered only by changing names to prevent the identification of individuals. These accounts should bring life to the examination and provide an intimate view of the crime. Such an approach will best address the objective of this study: the analysis of the dynamics and elements that make up parental child-stealing.

Arrest

Parental child-snatching is a low risk crime. In 79 percent (72) of the cases, offenders were not arrested or in custody at the time of the crime investigation. Only 21 percent (19) of the offenders were arrested. In no case was an additional felony beyond the child-theft included. The majority of child theft-investigations, 53 percent (48), were made by the Los Angeles Police Department. The Los Angeles County Sheriff's Department accounted for 23 percent (21) of the crimes reported, while a group of small, suburban police agencies reported 24 percent (22) of the snatchings to the district attorney.

The prosecution of child-stealing charges is greatly influenced by which law enforcement agency investigates the crime. When the frequency of prosecution is jointly viewed with the law enforcement agency reporting the offense, it is discovered that 52 percent (25) of the cases from the Los Angeles Police Department (LAPD) and 55 percent (12) of the smaller police agency cases were rejected for prosecution. In contrast, only 19 percent (4) of the Los Angeles County Sheriff's Department (LACSD) child-stealing reports were rejected for prosecution.

Such a difference between prosecution of law enforcement agency crime reports may be indicative of variations in reporting standards of individual officers, an officer's reluctance to intervene in a "family matter," or the quality of which crime investigations are completed.[1] Also, an officer may be reluctant to conduct a thorough investigation in which an offender is unavailable or unknown, especially if he or she suspects the crime to be the result of complex family relations. An informal screening or filtering process might be affecting the type of cases presented to the district attorney's office. LACSD may be very cautious in completing crime reports that, in turn, have greater prosecutorial merit when reviewed by the district attorney. The LAPD may be more responsive to victims' wishes and complete crime reports for a broader range of activities than the LACSD.

Geographic and demographic differences may have also affected the quality of such cases. The LAPD is restricted to service within the city of Los Angeles while the LACSD is responsible for unincorporated areas of the county and a variety of small independent cities that contract for LACSD service. And finally, there may be no factual basis for the present differences in filed or rejected cases of parental child-stealing. Such variations may be the result of natural reporting or activity patterns. Table 5-1 presents the filing or rejection of charges in terms of the law enforcement agency investigating the child-snatching.

Table 5-1
Parental Child-Stealing Case Filed or Rejected for Prosecution and Police Agency Reporting Crime

	Police Agency			
Prosecution Action	Los Angeles Police	Los Angeles Sheriffs	Other Police Departments	
Filed	23 (48%)	17 (81%)	10 (45%)	
Rejected	25 (52%)	4 (19%)	12 (55%)	
Column Total N	48	21	22	Total 91
%	(53)	(23)	(24)	100%

Prosecution of Criminal Charges

For a prosecutor in the Los Angeles County District Attorney's Office, the primary standard when screening parental child-stealing cases for prosecution is determining if the abduction is in violation of a custody order.[2] The initial desire is to settle the matter without creating a criminal action. This can be accomplished in two ways: first, through the use of a letter from the district attorney informing the offender of the law, urging return of the child, and indicating the possibility of criminal charges being initiated; second, through the use of mediation in the form of an office conference which may be sufficient to recover the child and rectify the case. Mediation is especially useful in cases in which a custody order is vague or violations are minor or infrequent. If a mediation session is impractical, the filing of criminal charges will follow.

The second policy step in responding to parental child-stealing is to initiate criminal misdemeanor prosecution. Misdemeanor complaints can be issued by the district attorney's office or the case will be referred to the city attorney for review and action.[3] Misdemeanor charges are usually indicative of less serious but more continuing domestic disharmony culminating in a child-theft. The final course of action is the filing of felony charges. Felony prosecutions are utilized in aggravated cases that might include a history of child-abductions or elaborate crime schemes, or when information indicates that the child was taken outside of California. If a child's whereabouts is unknown or the child is believed to be in another state, a felony charge is necessary to invoke extradition proceedings.

Every prosecuting attorney dealing with parental child-snatching expressed a desire to resolve the case by applying the minimum degree of action necessary. Their discretionary powers are very broad in screening such cases, but the prosecutors exercise prudent restraint in initiating criminal prosecutions. Since prosecution filing standards may vary among area offices within the district attorney's office, all or only selected aspects of the policy guidelines discussed above might be utilized.

Rejection of Criminal Charges

Of the 91 cases reviewed, child-stealing charges were filed in 55 percent (50) of the instances, while prosecution was rejected in 45 percent (41) of the cases. Of the forty-one cases rejected for prosecution of parental-child stealing, 32 percent (13) were rejected because of incomplete evidence to link the suspect with the crime, and 32 percent (13) were also referred to the Los Angeles City Attorney for misdemeanor prosecution. Charges were dismissed in the "interest of justice"[4] for 20 percent (8) of the rejected cases. The above three factors account for 84 percent (34) of the cases rejected for felony prosecution. Table 5-2 presents the basis for rejection of felony prosecution in parental child-stealing cases.

It should be recognized that cases rejected for prosecution because of incomplete evidence and referred for misdemeanor prosecution[5] may, in fact, be refiled and prosecuted successfully in a lower court jurisdiction. The present information system utilized by the district attorney's office precludes the tracking of cases through lower judicial districts. The prosecution of parental child-stealing offenses, when viewed broadly within the criminal justice system should increase beyond figures derived solely for prosecutions from the district attorney's office.[6]

The analysis of parental child-stealing cases screened for prosecution offers a good deal of information relating to the crime and circumstances surrounding the offense. The complex and sensitive nature of this crime and the relationships that create child-stealing can be acquired from the prosecutor's case summary justifying why a case is rejected for prosecution. The cases below illustrate the type of parental child-thefts usually rejected for criminal prosecution in Los Angeles County:

The following case describes a thirty-four-year-old father's theft of his eleven-year-old son and twelve-year-old daughter. Although the custodial parent has urged action by law enforcement to recover the children, she is uncooperative and will not file an official complaint.

> Susp. took children for visitation and did not return them. Ex spouse called police immediately following failure to return children. She demanded police pick up children who she assumed would still be with the Suspect in Malibu home. She does not wish Suspect arrested or prosecuted but asks only that police recover children. In view of refusal to prosecute by aggrieved party charges will not be filed.

Table 5-2
Reason Parental Child Stealing Case Rejected for Prosecution

Reason for Rejection	Number	Percent
Incomplete evidence	13	32
Misdemeanor—17B(4) referral	13	32
Dismissed—interest of justice	8	20
Improbability of conviction	3	7
Custodial parent requests no prosecution	1	2
Custodial parent unavailable/uncooperative	1	2
Affirmative defense	1	2
Other	1	2
Total	41[a]	99[b]

[a]Fifty cases were filed for prosecution.
[b]Error due to rounding.

The next case was dismissed in the interest of justice. A thirty-year-old father failed to return his two sons, aged twelve and fifteen, following court approved summer visitation privileges. The prosecutor has limited his involvement in this instance to issuing a letter to the offender as a means of inducing the return of both children.

> Vict. has custody rights to children. Suspect, the former husband, took children on visitation and failed to return them. Susp. has re-enrolled children in Visalia school system. At this stage of proceedings a prosecution is not deemed necessary. A letter will be sent to the suspect advising him that the visitation period has expired and that if the children are not returned charges will be filed.

The case below concerns a thirty-one-year-old mother's abduction of her ten-year-old daughter following weekend visitation. The case was rejected for felony prosecution and referred to the City Attorney for review as a misdemeanor offense:

> Natural mother takes child on 9-23-77 and does not return child per arrangement on 9-25-77. Child still missing on 10-5-77. Custody w/father. Mother entitled to reasonable visitation (not specified). Mother & her new husband have moved & have no forwarding address. Case does not warrant felony filing at this time. No showing of V being taken out of state. Resubmit if evidence located to show fleeing State.

The next case was rejected for prosecution because of the improbability of conviction. A three-year-old son was abducted by this twenty-three-year-old father. The father was very concerned that the home environment created by the mother, which included a cohabitation relationship and the use of narcotics, would be detrimental to his son's welfare:

> Police report reflects that Suspect went to ex-wife's house and took 3 year old son for visitation and has not returned. Child decree mentions reasonable visitation rights. Suspect took child because ex-wife was not caring for the boy. The ex-wife is apparently living with 2 males and also taking narcotics.

The final example of cases rejected for criminal prosecution depicts a twenty-nine-year-old father's theft of his four-year-old son following a one-week court-sanctioned visit. Because the mother is residing in a drug halfway house the father perceived this setting as harmful to the child. The boy was soon returned to his mother and the case was dismissed in the interest of justice:

> Father took child from mother who was living in a drug halfway house. He was concerned about safety of the child. Civil placement of child is pending. Father voluntarily returned child to custody of mother. No need for prosecution.

These case rejection summaries illustrate the complex web of family relations that prosecutors must untangle when prosecuting parental child-stealing crimes. The interaction of emotional, social, and legal elements within child-snatchings creates a delicate situation for prosecutors. For some case summaries, the prosecutor appears inordinately patient and disinterested in initiating criminal procedures. In other cases, prosecutors appear to disregard the custodial parent's claim to custody.

Bail

The amount of bail imposed upon parental child-stealers is generally low. Information concerning bail was available for forty-six of the offenders. Bail below twenty-five hundred dollars was required for 30 percent (14) of the offenders. Most offenders, 52 percent (23), received bail between thirty-five hundred and five thousand dollars. Only 17 percent (8) of the offenders received bail in excess of ten thousand dollars. The range of bail imposed upon the forty-six offenders was between one thousand dollars and twenty-five thousand dollars.

Final Disposition

Child-stealing cases are unlikely to be settled by judicial action. The final disposition (or last proceeding point)[7] found that in 23 percent (21) of the ninety-one cases examined, a bench warrant for the offender's arrest was issued. In 17 percent (15) of the cases, the charge was reduced to a misdemeanor offense. The case was dismissed in the interest of justice in 10 percent (9) of the instances. The custodial parent or essential witness refused to prosecute the offender in 5 percent (5) of the instances. Surprisingly, in only 14 percent (13) of the thefts was a guilty determination obtained. Table 5-3 presents the disposition for the cases studied.

The refusal of custodial parents to prosecute the offending party appears to be based upon two factors: first, the primary desire to reacquire the child through the most expedient means, and, second, compassion for the offending ex-spouse.

Parental child-stealing is a painful and traumatic experience. Custodial parents will, therefore, desire responsive and forceful action by the justice system to intimidate the offender. A custodial parent may seek the assistance of the district attorney's office with no commitment to complete criminal prosecution but as a threat to induce the offender to return the child quickly.

Once the child is returned to the guardian parent, that parent's withdrawal from criminal prosecution might be rooted in a desire to reduce

Table 5-3
Final Disposition of Parental Child-Stealing Cases

Disposition	Number	Percent
Arrest warrant issued	21	23
Misdemeanor referral—17B(4) reduced	15	17
Dismissed—interest of justice	9	10
Custodial parent/witness refused prosecution	5	5
Incomplete/insufficient evidence	13	14
Plea as charged or as lesser offense	9	10
Guilty/nolo contendre	4	4
Other evidence problems	6	7
Other disposition	9	10
Total	91	100

hostility in further relations with the ex-spouse. The following case depicts an offender's travel from New York to California and the theft of his seven-year-old daughter from school. The offender and child were located in New York and returned to relatives, at which time the custodial parent withdrew from prosecution in California. The police report with the custodial parent's statement refusing to cooperate in prosecution states:

> Reporting Party—Stated she was divorced from susp. in New York 2 years ago & has legal custody of vict. Stated approx. 2 wks ago susp came to Calif. to visit vict. at this time susp. broke into RP's residence and a police report was made. RP cancelled the police rpt. not wanting to prosecute her ex-husband. R stated since the abv rpt was made susp had made numerous phone calls, & come to visit. RP stated on 2-10-77 vict was attending school. RP was notified to come to the abv school, that a man fitting susp(s) desc had taken victim from the school playground. W-1 stated on 2-10-77 approx 1015 hrs her asst obs a M/W fitting susps desc, walking on the sidewalk adjacent to the school looking in at the children. W-1 stated it appeared the susp was looking for his child. W-1 later obs susp at the school exit holding vict. Wit then heard vict cry out "help" & obs susp running down the sidewalk w/vict.

> On 5-17-78 RP was contacted who stated that the susp was taken into custody by New York City police and her child was given to the custody of grandmother. Susp was subsequently released by New York Police.

> I NO LONGER WISH TO PROSECUTE MY EX-HUSBAND FOR TAKING MY DAUGHTER TO NEW YORK WITHOUT MY PERSMISSION.

Compassion toward the offenders may also account for custodial parents' failure to complete criminal prosecutions. They might rationalize the criminal actions as inappropriate between former spouses. The previous marital relationship and possible present relations with relatives would neutralize their desire to "send my ex-husband to jail" as one prosecutor was informed. Such compassion for the offender also indicates that although the marriage has been dissolved by divorce the parties recognize that they must continue to cooperate as parents. Parental roles requiring interaction between ex-spouses and the acknowledgment of a previous intimate relationship influence custodial parents to extend forgiveness to offenders by withdrawing from criminal proceedings. The following case which describes the theft of a ten-year-old son by his thirty-six-year-old father was refused for prosecution by the mother. The prosecuting attorney's summary note states:

> R stated she was given custody of son in her 1977 divorce. Her ex-husband went to Bridge St. School on 4-4-78 & took her son from school. Her son has not returned to school since. V teacher stated to R that V's father came to school & asked to talk to V. V didn't return to class. Teachers name unk.
>
> Child has been returned and mother has signed statement requesting no prosecution.

A custodial parent's withdrawal from prosecution can create a tenuous situation. Offenders recognize that custodial parents who refuse to prosecute are less likely to illicit responsive action in the future. Because the custodial parent might be viewed with diminished credibility, criminal justice personnel would be reticent in providing future assistance. Recognizing this, offenders might be motivated to attempt a second and more elaborate parental child-theft.

Extradition

Extradition between sister states is possible to assist in the prosecution of parental child-stealing offenses. The governor of each state makes a case-by-case determination to approve or deny the return of a suspect to another state. Guidelines for granting extradition in international flight cases are established on the federal level. No extradition requests from foreign nations are presently being approved for parental child-stealing offenses. This is based on the fact that parental child-snatching is exempt from international treaties. This policy applies regardless of the nature of the child theft or the specifications of a custody order. The kidnaping of children by nonparents will, however, have international extradition possibilities.

The use of interstate extradition to secure offenders for prosecution is rarely utilized in parental child-stealing crimes. In only 22 percent (20) of the cases studied was a request for extradition to California used. Child-stealing offenders who flee California are most likely to be extradited from Idaho, as found in 18 percent (4) of such cases. Ohio, Missouri, and Florida each accounted for 9 percent (2) of the extradition requests to return offenders to California for prosecution. The remaining extradition requests were distributed over a broad range of states.

One case was discovered of an extradition request to return an offender from a foreign country for prosecution. Although the request was rejected, the theft of a three-year-old boy by his mother and their flight to Venezuela illustrates the difficulties posed in locating parties involved in such crimes. The flight appears to be the result of numerous incidents of violence and a continuing hostility between the ex-spouses over custody of the child. The police report below provides a detailed account of the event:

> Vict. stated that on 9-2-77 Susp. picked up her son on agreement of a Court order. Susp. was to return son on 9-6-77 but failed to do so. Vict. went to Suspt's residence on 9-7-77 but no one answered. Vict. waited til 9-9-77 and again went to the resid. Vict. again was unable to get anyone to answer the door. Vict. called PD and they responded and contacted the MNGR. who opened the apt. Vict. and Ofcrs. discovered all of Suspt's personal items gone. The MNGR. informed Vict. that Susp. had moved, but didn't leave a forwarding address. Bet. 9-9-77 & 9-28-77 Vict. has called Susp's friends & gone to friends resid. to locate his son. Vict. also called Susp's family in Venezuela but was told that Susp. or son was not there. Vict. unable to locate Susp. or his son.

> I/O contacted Attorney for Susp. who stated that Susp. had in fact left the Country with the child "more than a month ago". That he did have an address for Susp. in Venezuela. Attorney stated that Susp. & V/R divorce has been a bitterly contested divorce primarily over custody of the child. Stated he would repeat what Susp. had told him—that Susp. had brought her father over from Venezuela to help her after the divorce—that she and her father were almost forced off the road on one occasion by another car driven by two male Latins—a few days later while in a telephone booth the same two Latins displayed a knife and told her something about that she should not care for the child. She also received phone calls from Latin men—Attorney stated Susp. believed these men had been hired by Vict. and was in great fear for her life. He stated Susp. had also told him that Vict. had beaten her on several occasions. I/O asked if Attorney had ever seen marks/injuries on Susp. Stated he had been shown photographs of injuries sustained to Susp's head & face which occurred in 1976—Also that Susp. had complained to the police on several occasions re: beatings by her husband but had been told nothing could be done.

> I/O located eight other crime reports filed by the (family name) 1976/77 not including this report. 11-1-77 matter submitted to DDA who issued felony warrant/extradition.

It can be assumed that a portion of the cases moving no further than the issuance of a bench warrant for the offender's arrest concern interstate flight. The number of extradition requests by the district attorney's office would increase provided that necessary information were available to complete extradition in child-snatching cases.

Sentences

The sentencing of individuals convicted of parental child-stealing creates particularly difficult problems for judges. Parental child-stealers do not have long criminal histories and have rarely been involved in serious crime. On the contrary, the child-snatchers are generally stable, responsible, and otherwise law abiding individuals.

The types of offenders and situational characteristics in parental child-stealing make each case unique when sentencing is necessary. What of the offender who takes his or her child for a relatively short period, who is remorseful, and who appears to pose no threat of abducting the child in the future? What degree of punishment is due an abductor who has secreted his or her child for the past six years, established a pattern of evading law enforcement, and exhibited a contempt for the criminal justice systems meddling into family matters? Judges must, therefore, grapple with the question of how much punishment is necessary to induce an offender to abide by the provisions within a child custody order.

A lenient sentence might induce an offender to disregard the law in the future. Offenders may perceive a benign sentence as an indication that the criminal justice system is not seriously concerned with upholding child custody decrees. The extent of punishment would not be sufficient, therefore, to restrain individuals desirous of the possession of their children from engaging in parental child-stealing.

Severe punishment of parents who steal their children may, however, provoke or further antagonize those persons to devise better crime schemes. A harsh punishment might be viewed as the ultimate intrusion by the justice system into a private or "family problem." For those individuals one might speculate that even extremely severe punishments would be ineffective in deterring future attempts at parental child-stealing.

Information regarding sentences for offenders found guilty of parental child-stealing was available for all thirteen cases. Of this group, 46 percent (6) received a sentence of some type of probation—23 percent (3) received formal probation and 23 percent (3) received summary probation. A sentence of both jail and probation was imposed on 38 percent (5) of these offenders, while 8 percent (1) received a sentence of a fine and 8 percent (1) were sentenced to county jail. In no instance did an offender receive a state prison sentence for parental child-stealing. The maximum fine imposed upon offenders was five hundred dollars. Formal probation periods did not exceed three years while summary probation sentences ranged up to five years. The longest county jail sentence was 180 days.

The present data indicates that parental child-stealing often circumvents the criminal justice system. Rarely are offenders arrested. Slightly more than half of the cases screened by the district attorney are filed for prosecution.

The prosecution of child-stealing offenses is hampered by the inability to locate the offender while many cases are prosecuted as misdemeanors. It is rare for an offender to be judged guilty, and sentences usually involve only probation.

Notes

1. This coincides with a previous study. See Peter Greenwood et al., *Prosecution of Adult Felony Defendants in Los Angeles County: A Policy Perspective* (Santa Monica: Rand Corporation, 1973).

2. See Los Angeles County District Attorney's Office, *Child Stealing Report*, August, 1977.

3. This is a matter of jurisdiction mandated by statute.

4. The classification "Dismissed in the Interest of Justice" according to PROMIS may include the following: time problems in prosecutor's action, search and seizure difficulties, case nonjustifiable, immunity to be provided, or a more applicable reason for rejection of charges was not given.

5. Misdemeanor referrals are usually under Cal. Penal Code secs. 17b-4-5.

6. See Michael W. Agopian, "Problems in the Prosecution of Parental Child-Stealing Offenses" (Paper presented at the Western Society of Criminology Conference, Newport Beach, California, 1980).

7. The last proceeding point indicates at which court event an action takes place. It is the final action, but not necessarily the disposition of the case. It can include the following: preliminary hearing, motion hearing, arraignment, issuing of bench warrant, or trial. Such actions are not conventionally viewed as final dispositions but provide the most current action available for cases in this study.

6

Participants in Parental Child-Stealing

The analysis of offenders and victims involved in criminal behavior generally deals with attempts to establish interlinkages between strangers. Crimes such as robbery, forcible rape, and aggravated assault usually concern individuals who are unrelated. But persons involved in parental child-stealing are an especially interesting group of individuals. In few criminal undertakings do the crime participants have such intimate knowledge of one another. It is this knowledge and the prior relationship between the parties which creates an unusually complex set of events that culminates in parental child-abductions.

Basic to understanding the sensitive and intricate crime situation in child-snatching is a clear portrait of those persons participating in this activity. Parental child-stealing requires three key individuals: the offender who is the noncustodial parent; the parent who is specified in a custody order as the child's guardian; and the victim who is abducted.

The present section charts a demographic profile of persons participating in parental child-stealing. It examines the differences between offenders and custodial parents on the basis of race, sex, age, marital status, and employment patterns. The target of the crime, the abducted child, is profiled on the basis of singular or multiple victims, race, sex, and the age of children abducted. And perhaps most important of all, the location of children snatched by a noncustodial parent is examined.

The Offender and the Custodial Parent

The racial composition of offenders and custodial parents clearly indicates that Caucasians are largely involved in parental child-stealing. They comprised 68 percent (62) of the offenders and 69 percent (63) of the custodial parents. Blacks made up 14 percent (13) of the offenders and 11 percent (10) of the custodial parents. Mexican-Americans accounted for 17 percent (15) of the abductors and 14 percent (13) of the custodial parents. Orientals comprised 1 percent (1) of the offenders and 6 percent (5) of the custodial parents. Interracial relationships between offenders and custodial parents was noted in 11 percent (10) of the cases. Table 6-1 presents the race of offenders and custodial parents.

Table 6-1
Race of Custodial Parent and Offender in Parental Child-Stealing

Race	Custodial Parent		Offender	
	Number	Percent	Number	Percent
Caucasian	63	69	62	68
Black	10	11	13	14
Mexican-American	13	14	15	17
Oriental	5	6	1	1
Total	91	100	91	100

One striking aspect of this profile of offenders and custodial parents from Los Angeles is the relatively low number of blacks and Mexican-Americans engaging in parental child-stealing. A number of factors might account for this finding. Black men have traditionally supported a strong mother role in the care of children. They would be much less likely to challenge a custody determination favoring the mother. Elliot Liebow, in his classic account of blacks in Washington, D.C., for instance, has noted how black ex-spouses display an unusual propensity to remain amenable toward each other following divorce.[1] Rarely did custodial mothers in his account hold child visitation privileges back as a bargaining chip to prompt child support payments from ex-spouses. And Liebow further noted the continued contact fathers upheld with their children following divorce. Black fathers, relinquishing the daily responsibilities of parenting to mothers, would shower their children with attention and gifts during visitation periods. Devoid of the mundane duties of parenting, black fathers especially relished the status and pleasure from such intense but brief roles as parent. This deep rooted view of mothers as the primary parent responsible for child rearing would account for the benign representation of blacks in parental child-stealing.

Mexican-Americans were similarly rarely involved in parental child-abductions. This may be indicative of the fact that they tend to refrain from utilizing divorce as a method of resolving domestic disharmony. Their maintenance of the extended family structure as a support mechanism and strong religious convictions which discourage divorce would reduce the involvement of Mexican-Americans in child custody disputes. In addition, they usually subscribe to clear family role differentiations that would coincide with the common practice of courts almost always awarding custody of children to mothers.

Caucasians appear to place less emphasis upon the seriousness of violating judicial decrees. Their overwhelming representation in child-thefts is in marked contrast to their lesser participation in other forms of criminal behavior such as homicide, aggravated assault, or forcible rape.

Their battling over the custody of a child may be due, in part, to a reduced emphasis upon the traditional family structure. Caucasians tend to exhibit greater mobility and are representative of a more contemporary lifestyle. Their general isolation from support factors such as extended family or religious commitments might account for the greater representation of Caucasians in parental child-stealing. And finally, the large number of Caucasians engaging in child-snatching may be a natural extension of their participation in divorce and not indicative of any especially inflated patterns in settling child custody disputes by child-theft.

Fathers steal children twice as frequently as mothers. Males accounted for 71 percent (65) of the offenders in Los Angeles while females snatched their children in 29 percent (26) of the cases. It may appear axiomatic that child-snatchers are overwhelmingly males since custody awards almost exclusively favor mothers as the custodial parent. Although either parent can justify his actions, the dynamics that make for a parent abducting a child are often complex and rooted in the battle for custody and the process of awarding the child to a particular parent.

Traditionally, fathers have readily accepted the common practice of courts' awarding custody of children to the mother. The loss of contact with their children was all too frequently a distasteful corollary of divorce expected and accepted by fathers. Such custody determinations were usually based upon a deeply held yet unsubstantiated belief by judges that the mother was the superior parent. Enormous value was placed on the powers of maternal instinct which became a nearly impenetrable barrier for fathers seeking custody of their children. In very limited situations some fathers attempted to challenge custody awards where a concern for the physical welfare of the child could be established if the child was awarded to the mother. The following case describes a custodial mother's lifestyle which includes her cohabitation with two men, extensive drug use, and indiscriminate sexual activity.

The twenty-three-year-old offender's deep concern for his three-year-old son's physical and emotional welfare is vividly discussed with the investigating officer below:

> On 12-27-77 at approximately 2200 hours I made contact with the suspect (father). I informed him that I was conducting an investigation in a possible child stealing and I advised him of his Constitutional Rights and he stated he understood them as I had read them to him, and he desired to speak to me without having an attorney present during questioning.

> The suspect stated that he and his wife have been separated at different periods of time over the last two years. He stated that she was currently living with his ex-friend RAYMOND, RON and a 17 year old boy that he knew as 'TOM'. He stated that he had the child, his son, 'JUSTIN' for visitation over the Thanksgiving holidays and that he had returned him

after Thanksgiving Day. He stated that during this visitation the child had a severe rash around and about the lower portion of his body, and that he had bought medication for the baby's rash. He stated that approximately one week before Christmas on Saturday morning, he had made arrangements to pick up the child from his wife, 'CAROL' and that she had agreed that he pick the child up early in the morning on his way home from work. He stated that when he went to his wife's apartment he was allowed entry by 'TOM' and that he had picked up the child, however, the child was in an extremely filthy condition. He stated that he attempted to wake his wife by knocking on her bedroom door, to ascertain if there were any clean clothes for the child that he could take with him. He stated that he was unable to wake her, however, her boyfriend 'RON' told him through the closed bedroom door that he would attempt to wake her, however, he was unable to do so. The suspect stated that he then left and went to his home in Pomona where he subsequently bought clothes for the child. He stated that upon examining the child the rash that he had treated over the Thanksgiving holiday appeared to be worse and he purchased more medicine for the rash. He related that on several occasions he had been advised by friends who live in the apartment complex, that his wife was living with two males and that she had, on occasion, injected Cocaine in addition to smoking marijuana. He stated that he was advised that on one occasion his wife was having sexual intercourse with two males, unidentified, and that the child was in the same room and that the child had awakened and began crying. Stated that he was advised that one of the males slapped the child and told him to, "Shut up." I asked the suspect if he had ever seen bruises on his son when he visited him and he stated that he did not. Suspect stated to me at that time that the child was not at his residence, but was with someone who was caring for the child. He further stated that he could not, in good conscience, allow his child to go back into the atmosphere, that he had been living in with his mother, and that if he had to go to jail he would.

I then returned to the El Monte Police Department and I was contacted by telephone by CAROL (mother). I informed her that I had been to her husband's residence and that I needed to get statements from RON RAYMOND and TOM JOHNSON to complete the report. She stated that her boyfriend 'RON' would not come to the police department because she thought he had a warrant for his arrest and asked me if I would talk to him on the telephone. I informed her that I needed to talk to him in person, however, that I would talk to him on the phone. I then had a conversation with a male who identified himself as RON RAYMOND and he stated basically the same as CAROL (the mother), except that the occurrence had not been Thanksgiving Day, it had been approximately one week ago, indicating the date given by the suspect. The individual stated that he remembered when the suspect came into the apartment and that the suspect had knocked on the bedroom door and attempted to wake his wife CAROL. During the conversation with the individual it was difficult for me to understand his conversation, and from his voice it appeared that he was possibly intoxicated.

On 11-29-77 at approximately 1000 hours I was contacted again by complainant (CAROL) at the El Monte Police Department. She stated to me at that time that she had contacted the Los Angeles County Sheriff's De-

partment regarding the matter because she wanted, "something done." At
that time I advised her that I was conducting an investigation and I asked
her to step back into the interrogation room of the detective bureau trailer
so that I might talk to her in private. It should be noted that she had an
unidentified female with her. Upon entering the interrogation room I advised her of some of the statements made by her husband and that it was a
necessity to attempt to prove or disapprove his statements. I advised her
that he had stated that he injected Cocaine and I asked to see her arms.
She removed her coat and exposed the inner elbows of both arms and I
observed what appeared to be cites of illegal injections on both inner
elbows. She stated that the marks did not mean anything, that she had
marks all over her arms and hands, and I informed her that I had been
assigned as an undercover narcotic investigator while employed with the El
Monte Police Department, and that I had given expert testimony in
numerous Courts relative to illegal injections and narcotic violations. I
asked her if she also smoked marijuana, and she stated she usually smoked
two or three joints after she came home from work to, "unwind." I stated
to her again that, due to the conflicting statements given by her, and the
conflicting statements given by her and her husband, that I would complete
a formal report and submit it to the District Attorney's Office of the
County of Los Angeles for their consideration. I asked her if she was concerned about the child's safety or welfare while with his father, and she
stated that she was not, and that she felt the baby would be taken care of
properly, however, she wanted the baby back.

   In recent years, sex roles in America have undergone significant realign-
ment. One by-product of these changes is the expanded interest and participation of fathers in the responsibilities of parenting. When divorce
dissolves the marriage, fathers who have come to cherish their active parenting role are increasingly reluctant to relinquish custody of their children.
Fathers are now seeking custody of their children in increasingly larger
numbers. It appears that their efforts are being rewarded. Although no official statistics are available, most professionals agree that mothers generally retain custody of the child following divorce in about 90 percent of the
instances. The cases of parental child-stealing from Los Angeles, however,
indicate that in 29 percent of the cases fathers were awarded custody of the
child. One must project that this modest trend will continue and is a precursor for an even greater shift toward equalizing child custody awards between mothers and fathers.

   Mothers who lose custody of their children must deal with a more complex array of conditions than fathers. It might be expected that child-
snatching is a more easily induced and justified activity for female offenders. Because they are aware of the established tradition of granting
mothers custody, those females who lose guardianship of their children will
view such a determination as a judicial slap in the face. It subverts their role
expectations and personal desires. Because convention dictates that in only
the most detrimental and deficient instances will mothers lose custody of a

child, noncustodial mothers are placed in a particularly awkward position. Often the mother who is deprived custody will view the process of determining custody as being grossly biased and inadequate in assessing her parenting skills. The following comment by a thirty-nine-year-old female offender who has lost custody of her two sons, age eight and nine years, illustrates such a viewpoint. The father was successful in obtaining a change of custody, and the offender attempted to avoid returning the boys by moving to a rural area near Carmel, California. She was finally located and upon being presented with the new decree that awards custody to the father she stated:

> I will not to go Santa Cruz to appear before that fucking judge. I have no money, no car, and no one's going to take my kids away from me. If anyone tries I'll blow their fucking heads off. No mother in the State of California has been more hassled than me and no mother is a better mother to her children than me.

Another factor that may prompt noncustodial mothers into child-snatching is the belief that they are more capable of raising the child than the father. Female offenders who rationalize their crime on such a basis utilize a vast array of factors: they frequently note the limited time commitment of fathers due to work schedules, the difficulty a father might display in grappling with the daily responsibilities of child rearing, and that mystic element of maternal instinct which more effectively equips mothers for parenting. In such cases mothers are not establishing a child's endangerment or the father's gross deficiency in child rearing. They usually cannot establish any blatant harm done to the child. Mothers are emphasizing that they can provide a higher quality of homelife for their children and that their children's best interests will be served if they are the custodial parent. Mothers assert that fathers are depriving the child of a more meaningful parenting experience by retaining custody.

The following letter was sent by a thirty-eight-year-old mother after she abducted her four-year-old daughter from the custodial father. She fled to Texas with the child. The letter chronicles the tenuous position noncustodial mothers occupy, especially when a child expresses a desire to establish closer contact. Of particular importance is the variety of factors used by the offender to rationalize the crime. She notes the child's welfare, the attorney's recommendation that future litigation would be futile, her desire to raise the child, and the perceived emotional trauma of returning her daughter following visitation periods:

> Dear Jerry,
> I'm sorry for the hurt your going thru and the hurt we're going thru but I saw no other way. Cathy's life at your side was wrong and you didn't want

to change your way of life to make it adequate for her & I couldn't let her continue to beg me not to take her back to you. And I know she loves you too but she needed to be with me as much as I needed to be with her. Each time I had to force her to stay with you must have made her feel I didn't want her. I asked you to let me take care of her while you worked. I told you I could quit my job but you said no. It was getting harder and harder for her, with you having a different babysitter every other week depending who you were mad at. It was always hard for me to leave her but each attorney I saw gave me the same answer "there's no point in going to court again so long as he has her". I didn't want to do this. I don't want to hurt you. I do love you very much in spite of everything. When I called that Sunday to Angies I was gonna come back but you were gonna be mad & than Cathy said "please don't take me back to my papa he's gonna take me away from you" and she was crying and I told her I wouldn't take her back. I'm sorry. I tell her you love her. Thats why you want her to stay with you too & she sees your picture. She won't forget you nor hate you and she might have if things had remained as they were. I'm sorry for the hurt but she hurts less this way and her life is more stable. I would like for Cathy to talk with you on the phone but I don't know if this would hurt you more than not hearing at all. I'll call soon to Angies. If you really love her and it's not just a matter of owning you know she's better off then the life you gave her.

A noncustodial mother might also engage in child-snatching because of unusually stressful peer pressure. Mothers who lose custody of their children might be perceived as wantonly lacking in their parental responsibilities. The noncustodial mother's inducement to steal the child against a custody order may be spawned by her belief that the custodial father was particularly sophisticated or cunning during a custody dispute or that he maintained inequitable financial resources to more aggressively pursue a favorable custody award. Believing that their ex-husbands have slyly beat the traditional odds against retaining custody following divorce, mothers would be less inclined to obey a child custody decree.

The age distribution of participants indicates that both offenders and custodial parents are generally young and within the same age group. Most offenders, 35 percent (32), and most custodial parents, 35 percent (30), were between twenty-seven and thirty-one years of age. The next most common age group for offenders and custodial parents was between thirty-two and thirty-six years of age—25 percent (23) of the offenders and 22 percent (20) of the custodial parents. The youthfulness of participants in child-snatchings is evident since 73 percent (67) of the offenders and 77 percent (65) of the custodial parents were thirty-six years of age or younger. The mean age of offenders was thirty-four years, while the mean age of custodial parents was thirty-three. Ages of offenders ranged from twenty-two to sixty-six years of age, while the age range for custodial parents was between twenty-one and seventy-three years of age. Table 6-2 presents the age distribution for offenders and custodial parents participating in child-snatching.

Table 6-2
Age of Custodial Parent and Offender in Parental Child-Stealing

	Custodial Parent		Offender	
Age in Years	Number	Percent	Number	Percent
17 to 21	4	5	0	0
22 to 26	11	13	12	13
27 to 31	30	35	32	35
32 to 36	20	24	23	25
37 to 41	10	12	8	9
42 to 46	5	6	4	4
47 to 51	1	1	7	8
52 to 56	3	3	3	3
57 or more	1	1	2	2
Total	85[a]	100	91	99[b]

[a]Six missing cases.
[b]Error due to rounding.

Child-snatching occurs between persons whose relationship has been terminated by divorce. Of the offenders involved, 78 percent (71) were divorced, while 72 percent (65) of the custodial parents were divorced. Offenders reported being separated in 21 percent (19) of the cases, and custodial parents separated in 26 percent (23) of the instances. Cohabitation was rare for participants in child-stealing. One case of cohabitation was reported each for offenders and custodial parents. It should be recognized that the analysis of the participants' marital status concerns their present state and is differentiated from the relationship between participants. Remarriage or cohabitation with another person not the child's parent is, therefore, possible.

Employment information was available for fifty of the offenders and seventy-two of the custodial parents. Participants in child-stealing are usually employed—70 percent (35) of the offenders and 67 percent (48) of the custodial parents, but a surprisingly large number of offenders, 28 percent (14), and custodial parents, 21 percent (15), were discovered to be unemployed. Only one offender was a homemaker, while 10 percent of the custodial parents (7) were homemakers. One custodial parent reported being retired. It is most likely that many of the offenders for whom employment data was unavailable were in fact working. The relocation, support, and concealment of the abducted child would necessitate a stable source of income. Many offenders are also most probably being aided by relatives or friends who might channel financial assistance or directly aid in their concealment from authorities. Such assistance provides the vital necessities for continued mobility and a clandestine lifestyle: a car, home, or mail. And lastly, the large number of unemployed offenders might be an accurate indicator of offenders' employment status at the time of the crime. They may have resigned from a job just prior to the abduction and planned to reenter the work force once safely secreted from authorities.

The Victim

Children are truly the defenseless victims of this crime. The ninety-one offenders abducted 130 children from their custodial parents. The abduction of a lone child was most common, as reported in 64 percent (58) of the crimes. Two children were snatched in 30 percent (27) of the instances. Multiple child-thefts that ranged from two to five children in a single crime occurred in 36 percent (33) of the thefts.

White children are overwhelmingly the target of parental child-stealers. The children snatched were racially comprised of 74 percent (96) white, 11 percent (14) each of black and Mexican-American, and 5 percent (6) Oriental.

Male and female children are equally likely to be abducted from a parent. The sex of children snatched was comprised of 51 percent (66) males and 49 percent (64) females.

Young children are clearly the victims of parental child-thefts. Children between three and five years of age were most frequently snatched, as discoverd for 34 percent (44) of the children. Children between six and eight years of age were stolen in 22 percent (28) of the thefts, while those between nine and eleven years of age accounted for 26 percent (34) of the children abducted. Children twelve years of age or older comprised only 13 percent (11) of those snatched. The desire to steal young children becomes evident, since 87 percent (113) of the children were eleven years of age or younger. The mean age for children abducted by a parent was seven years. Table 6-3 presents the age distribution for children at the time of the theft.

Clearly, children between three and eleven years of age are the primary targets in parental child-thefts. Children below three years of age pose serious logistical problems for a single parent. They will require extensive supervision

Table 6-3
Age of Victim at Time of Offense

Age in Years	Number	Percent
6 months to 2 years	7	5
3 to 5	44	34
6 to 8	28	22
9 to 11	34	26
12 to 14	11	9
15 to 17	5	4
Total	129[a]	100

[a]One missing case.

and create problems or interferences for a single, working parent. And children over eleven years of age are too self-sufficient for a parent seeking to conceal their whereabouts. Unless continually supervised, adolescent children can telephone the custodial parent, notify law enforcement agencies, or seek transportation home.

Participants in parental child-stealing—excluding the present offense—appear to be conventional and void of any patterns of previous criminal activity. The child-theft is generally the most serious law violation for participants. Following the abduction, offenders desire to resume a stable but clandestine home environment. Such episodic law violators pose especially difficult problems for resolving child custody disputes. With no proclivity toward committing additional crime, these individuals are well insulated from contact with law enforcement authorities. For offenders who have abducted a child and integrated into a new community, contact with law enforcement authorities because of some minor offense—usually vehicle infractions or inspections at border crossings—becomes the most eminent form of detection. The profile of participants in parental child-stealing, therefore, is of an individual who is Caucasian, generally young, frequently employed, and with a crime-free history.

One of the most important concerns in parental child-stealing is the reunion of guardian and child. The number of children reunited with custodial parents does not lead to optimism. In only 47 percent (43) of the cases examined was the child returned to the legal guardian. In 5 percent (5) of the instances, the child was only located, while in one instance the child was placed into protective custody until custody could be verified and travel arrangements to California completed.

The chances for the return or location of abducted children are enhanced when custodial parents notify law enforcement personnel of the crime early. Most custodial parents that had children returned, that is, 41 percent (14), informed authorities within one week of the crime. Children were returned in 45 percent (9) of the instances when custodial parents notified authorities between eight and thirty days of the crime, while 36 percent (8) of the children returned had parents who informed authorities of the theft on the day of the occurrence. Parents who fail to quickly notify authorities of the abduction leave a cold trail for law enforcement to follow and thereby seriously reduce the probability of locating the child. Table 6-4 jointly views the number of days between offense and reporting to authorities with the return or location of the snatched child.

It is interesting to note that in 80 percent (20) of the instances in which a child was returned or located, the offender and custodial parent utilized communication by telephone. In 12 percent (3) of the cases in which a child was returned or located, communication between offender and custodial parent was in person, and in 8 percent (2) of such cases, the participants

Table 6-4
Location or Return of Child, and Days between Offense and Reporting to Police

Location or Return	Days between Offense and Reporting to Police			
	Same Day	1 to 7 Days	8 to 30 Days	31 or More Days
Not returned or located	13 (59%)	8 (53%)	9 (45%)	12 (80%)
Located only	1 (5%)	1 (3%)	2 (10%)	1 (7%)
Returned to custodial parent	8 (36%)	14 (41%)	9 (45%)	2 (13%)
Placed into protective custody	0 (0%)	1 (3%)	0 (0%)	0 (0%)
Total N	22	34	20	15
%	(100)	(100)	(100)	(100)

communicated by mail. The eventual return of the child that included direct communication between the ex-spouses may indicate a sincere concern for the care of the child or even the use of the crime situation as a forum to discuss the ruptured marital relationship. In 43 percent (39) of the cases, therefore, the victim was returned to the custodial parent, placed into protective custody, or simply located.

A recovery rate of less than 50 percent for victims of parental child-stealing is most distressing. One might suspect that the recovery rate for stolen automobiles or lost pets is substantially greater. There are, of course, logistical difficulties in locating child-theft victims. Their dependence on and trust in a parent would preclude any escape attempt, identification features such as hair color or name can be easily altered, and the fact that offenders are consciously evading authorities are just a few of the impediments to locating victims of parental child-abductions. Additional information from the offenders themselves concerning the process, aid received from others, and the fugitive lifestyle will be most valuable in more accurately assessing the difficulty of locating children victimized by child-snatching.

Note

1. Elliot Liebow, *Tally's Corner* (Boston: Little, Brown & Company, 1967).

7 Temporal Patterns of Parental Child-Stealing

The analysis of parental child-stealing to assess seasonal and other temporal variations may yield valuable linkages to understanding the crime. Are the abductions perpetrated without clear temporal considerations, or is there a pattern according to mornings or evenings? Are they more common during weekends, school holidays, or summer vacations? The following section examines the temporal aspects of parental child-thefts.

Month of Year of Crime

The charting of child-stealing crimes by month of year shows that they are well distributed throughout all seasons of the year. When the year was divided into four seasons, it was discovered that parental child-thefts occurred in 30 percent (27) of the cases during the fall, 29 percent (26) during the summer, 21 percent (19) during winter, and 20 percent (19) during the spring season. Most child-snatchings took place during April and September—each accounting for 13 percent (12) of the crimes. May was the least likely month for a parental child-theft, with only 2 percent (2) of the offenses studied occurring in that month. Table 7-1 presents the distribution of parental child-abductions by month of year.

The distribution of parental child-thefts by season of the year fails to indicate any consistent pattern. Offenders generally find each season equally attractive for the crime. The slightly larger number of offenses during the fall and summer seasons may be linked with child custody orders. Custody decrees frequently specify that a child be with the noncustodial parent during the summer months or for an extended visitation period during the summer. If a child has been returned to the custodial parent following a particularly pleasant summer visitation, the noncustodial parent may have a clear recollection of that experience. Many crimes during the fall might be induced by the summer visitation recently completed and the offender's desire to continue a full-time parent-child relationship. Summer offenses can be the result of noncustodial parents' refusing to return the child at the termination of the extended summer visitation period.

Table 7-1
Parental Child-Stealing Offenses by Month of Year

Month	Number	Percent
January	8	9
February	5	5
March	5	5
April	12	13
May	2	2
June	9	10
July	8	9
August	9	10
September	12	13
October	7	8
November	8	9
December	6	7
Total	91	100

Day of Week of Crime

Child-thefts usually take place during the weekend days. Fridays were found to be the most perilous day, with 21 percent (19) of the crimes, followed by Saturday and Sunday, each recording 16 percent (15) of the offenses. The weekend days—Friday, Saturday, and Sunday—accounted for 53 percent (49) of all parental child-abductions. The mid-week days were the safest from snatchings, with Tuesday noting only 7 percent (6) and Thursday 10 percent (9) of the crimes. Table 7-2 presents the day of the week on which parental child-thefts were committed.

The large number of child-thefts during the weekend may be explained by the fact that most custody decrees specify weekends as the visitation period for the noncustodial parent. Although a visitation parent has guardianship of the child through the weekend, Friday may be reported as the

Table 7-2
Parental Child-Stealing Offenses by Day of Week

Day of Week	Number	Percent
Sunday	15	16
Monday	13	14
Tuesday	6	7
Wednesday	14	15
Thursday	9	10
Friday	19	21
Saturday	15	16
Total	91	99[a]

[a]Error due to rounding.

final day that the custodial parent possessed the child. Also, in cases in which no visitation privilege is specified, offenders may find the weekend, especially Friday, a particularly convenient time in which to perpetrate the crime. The child will be in transit, often moving openly to or from school. The weekend will provide a buffer in which to travel and relocate into a new community or to find employment for the offender. The following case illustrates a thirty-year-old father's use of the court approved visitation period to abduct his two daughters, aged six and three years, from his twenty-eight-year-old ex-spouse. The investigating officer's crime report states:

> We responded to the location Re a child stealing report call and were advised by the victim that her ex-husband picked up her two daughters for the weekend and was to return Sunday 4-9-78 at 1700 hrs.

> When the Suspect did not return the victim states she made some phone calls to Santa Barbara where her ex-husband lives, and found out that he had sold all of his financial holdings and has left the area.

> The victim states that he has approx. $500,000 in cash and may leave the state or country. The victim has a court order in her possession proclaiming her the legal guardian of the above children with her ex-husband having normal weekend visitation rights.

The use of court sanctioned visitation periods places the custodial parent in a precarious position. One violates the law by refusing the non-custodial parent mandated visitation privileges yet inadvertently supports the crime plan by providing a predictable and nonthreatening means for the offender to gain possession of a child. The next case summary describes how an offender's compliance with weekend visitation privileges over an extended period was turned into an opportunity to abduct his five-year-old daughter:

> R/P relates that on 10-14-77 at 1500 hrs. abv Susp. her X husband, picked up missing child for the weekend. Susp. never returned the child. R/P learned approx. 2 wks ago that Susp. and her daughter were suppose to be in Tahoe, Calif. R/P went to Tahoe and checked all the schools and, also, with Susps. friends. No child or x-husband. Approx. 2 days ago Susp. called R/P's mother and told her that he was in Tahoe, Calif. Susp had been picking up his daughter every Friday around 1500 hrs. and bringing her back on Sundays around 2000 hrs.

Monday crimes may be an appendage to weekend thefts. Since weekend visitation usually extends until Sunday, the reporting of an abduction may be postponed until the following morning. Friday, Saturday, Sunday, and Monday reports account for 69 percent (62) of the child thefts. Also, a disproportionate number of holidays occur on Monday, and visitation privileges are often linked to holidays. The following account of a father refusing to return his thirteen-year-old daughter depicts the preciseness with which custody decrees are linked to holidays:

> Wit., Victs. legal guardian stated her ex-husband picked up vict. (her daughter) for visitation per court order. Susp. stated he would ret. vict. the same day (2-12-78) at 1900 hrs. To date Vict has not been return to Wit.
>
> Final judgment of divorce decree dated April 27, 1967 gave the following provisions for visitation: "that the defendant (Susp) has the right of reasonable visitation with the minor children of the parties, and the privilege of having the children with him for a period of one-half of the summer school vacation period, and further, that the defendant shall give the plaintiff at least thirty days advance notice of his intention to exercise the summer visitation privileges, and fifteen days advance notice of his intention to exercise the Easter and Christmas school vacation periods". The above refusal of Susp. is not covered by any of the above.

The incorporation of child-thefts into holiday visits is extremely convenient for offenders. Offenders can gain the trust of parental victims by complying with a custody order for a moderate period. When visitations are extended over holidays or the summer periods, a noncustodial parent might initiate legal proceedings in another jurisdiction as illustrated by the following case. The report describes the fourth such attempt by the thirty-four-year-old ex-husband to detain the two children, a son age nine and a daughter age ten years, beyond the court designated visitation period. The mother's daring attempt to resteal the children and the enormous logistical problems surrounding the reacquisition of stolen children in interstate cases is cogently described:

> The victim/informant stated that the two children who went to visit their father over the Thanksgiving holiday have not been returned home by him. The victim and the father are divorced. The court in Clayton, MO, granted custody of the two children to the victim (mother). The father was granted visitation rights.
>
> On 11-23-77, at approx. 0030 hours, the victim placed the two children on a TWA flight to St. Louis, Missouri, at L.A. International Airport. She confirmed their arrival in St. Louis, MO when she talked to them over the phone. She was told at this time that the children would return to L.A. International Airport on 11-27-77 at approx. 2021 hours, flight #269. The victim went to the airport and was informed that the children had not arrived at LAX.
>
> She called her ex-husband in St. Louis, MO, wanting to know where the children were. The ex-husband answered that they were there with him and he was going to keep them until he went to court to get custody of the two children. The victim called her ex-husband again at 0600 11-28-77 to try to talk to the children. The ex-husband refused to let the children talk to her, telling the victim to call back in a couple of days.

The victim indicated that she had a court order, signed by the St. Louis County Court, granting her custody of the children, specifying what the terms of visitation were to be. The terms of visitation in the court order were as follows: Susp. was to have visitation rights for two (2) months during the Summer and on alternating national holidays for the weekend, which include Saturday, Sunday and the holiday. The order also granted custody to Susp. for one-half of the day for Christmas and Thanksgiving. On April 14, 1974 the court order was amended granting Susp. custody of the children for one half of the Christmas vacation, alternate three day holidays and Spring vacation, with the condition that he pay all travel costs.

The victim wants to press charges against the ex-husband on the grounds that she is the legal guardian of the children and that the ex-husband is keeping the children against their wishes and the orders of the court.

I made contact with V/I about the re-taking of her children. She related the following:

On 12-12-77 at about 6:00 p.m. she and her husband arrived in St. Louis. They rented a car and drove to the Suspect's residence, St. Louis, MO. At the Suspect's residence they observed Suspect exit the house and go to a vehicle parked in the driveway. Suspect opened both front doors to the vehicle and then returned to the house. A few minutes later Suspect and the two children came out of the house and started across the yard to the vehicle. Upon observing the V/I, Suspect pushed the two children into the vehicle and closed the door. The children upon observing their mother, R/P, exited the other side and ran crying to their mother.

At this time Suspect jumped V/I's husband and knocked him to the ground, and a scuffle took place. During the scuffle V/I requested a neighbor to call the police. Upon arrival of the police Suspect and V/I's husband were taken into custody for disturbing the peace. The children were then detained for their own protection.

After V/I produced a certified copy of the custody order the children were released to her custody.

Time of Day of Crime

The most hazardous hours for parental child-stealing are the late afternoon and early evening periods. To examine the distribution for time of day of the crime, quarterly periods of six hours each were used. The greatest number of thefts, 43 percent (39), was found between 2:00 P.M. and 7:59 P.M. The morning and early afternoon quartile of 8:00 A.M. to 1:59 P.M. accounted for the second most common time period of thefts, with 40 percent (36) of the crimes occurring at that time. The least dangerous time period for child-stealing was during the early morning hours of 2:00 A.M. to 7:59 A.M., which accounted for only 7 percent (6) of the offenses. Child-abductions by time of day are displayed in table 7-3.

Table 7-3
Parental Child-Stealing Offenses by Time of Day

Time of Day	Number	Percent
2:00 A.M. to 7:59 A.M.	6	7
8:00 A.M. to 1:59 P.M.	36	40
2:00 P.M. to 7:59 P.M.	39	43
8:00 P.M. to 1:59 A.M.	10	11
Total	91	101[a]

[a]Error due to rounding.

Such a time distribution for child-snatchings may reflect the fact that the child will be in public for an extended period of time. He or she may be in transit from school to home, toward a playground, or, if the custodial parent is employed, in a temporary care facility. Thefts during the morning hours may be a result of most day visitations being initiated during these hours. The offender may utilize the day visitation as an opportunity for child-stealing. The theft of three children aged ten, eleven, and thirteen years by their forty-five-year-old father which occurred under the pretense of a court approved day visitation order is reported below. The offender arrogantly announced that he was going into hiding with the children and also voiced his displeasure with the ex-wife's dating:

> Informant was contacted at the complaint counter of A.V. station by the reporting deputy. Informant stated suspect arrived at location at approx. 10:00 am in the listed Cadillac. Their three children met him at the driveway and entered the Cadillac, and they left location. By prearrangement Suspect was to have the children for the day. Approximately one hour later, Suspect called informant collect and stated he was not going to bring the kids back tonight and he was taking them on a vacation and he intended to keep them indefinitely. Informant also stated Suspect was angry because she was dating other men.

> Informant believes Suspect is in the process of moving from Townhouse Motel to Rancho Mirage Trl. Park. It is unknown at this time where Suspect & children are, or where Suspect intends to take them.

Temporal patterns for parental child-stealing clearly illustrate the offender's opportunity to use court prescribed visitation periods as a means to take possession of the child. This allows offenders to plan the abduction and places the custodial parent in a precarious situation when surrendering a child for visitation privileges.

Days between Crime and Custody Order

When the period between a parental child-theft and the custody decree or divorce was examined, it was discovered that most crimes, 55 percent (49), occur within eighteen months of a custody order or divorce action. However, the single largest number of offenses, 37 percent (26), occurred two years after the divorce. This was followed by 23 percent (16) of the thefts occurring between six to twelve months after the custody order or divorce while 18 percent (13) of the child snatchings took place within six months of a custody decree or divorce. Table 7-4 presents the distribution for parental child-thefts by days between the crime and custody order or divorce.

The noncustodial parent's compliance with visitation conditions for a moderate length of time enhances the possibility of success of a crime scheme. Trust of the custodial parent is gained which may induce him or her to delay reporting the crime to law enforcement agencies. Acquiring possession of the child will also be predictable and without suspicion. This period of compliance, therefore, may be an essential preparatory element of the crime plan or may represent accumulated frustration with the visitation arrangement. Such a finding supports the position that parental child-thefts are an extension of court approved visitation periods.

Table 7-4
Days between Offense and Issuance of Child-Custody Order

Days between Crime and Custody Order	Number	Percent
0 to 181 days (6 months)	13	18
181 to 365 days (12 months)	16	23
366 to 546 days (18 months)	10	14
547 to 727 days (24 months)	5	7
730 or more days (over 2 years)	26	37
Total	70[a]	99[b]

[a]No information for 21 cases.
[b]Error due to rounding.

8

Situational Characteristics and Modus Operandi of Parental Child-Stealing

Of special importance in understanding the dynamics of parental child-stealing is an examination of the process that enables a noncustodial parent to seize control of the child. How is an offender placed in a setting that allows access to the child? Are certain opportunities more inviting than others for commission of the child-snatching? What are the interactional ingredients between participants immediately prior to the crime?

If a parental child-theft is an unannounced surprise seizure of a child from a public location, then the offender must create his own opportunity for the crime. But an offender may utilize the unsuspecting custodial parent as an auxiliary resource in the formula for gaining possession of the child. A noncustodial parent with specified visitation periods can develop a convenient arena for abducting the child and departing from the crime scene. Such a forum would be particularly attractive for reestablishing the offender and child into a new school, job, and community, all of which are vital to insuring anonymity from authorities. An analysis of the situational elements immediately preceding the child-snatching can clarify how the offender takes physical possession of the victim.

Precipitating Circumstances

Most child thefts, 33 percent (30), were perpetrated under the guise of an ex-spouse's exercising weekend visitation privileges. The second most popular medium for seizing a child was from a babysitter, as noted in 16 percent (15) of the cases. Day visitation privileges were used in 12 percent (11) of the thefts, while a variety of other means accounted for 21 percent (20) of the abductions. Table 8-1 presents the precipitating circumstances that led to the offender's gaining possession of the child in each of the cases studied.

It is relatively easy to gain control of a child. In 55 percent (50) of the cases, the offender used a court-approved visitation period to seize possession of a child for purposes of child-snatching. An offender can employ a variety of mediums to gain temporary possession of a child and simply refuse to relinquish the child after the expiration of the sanctioned period. The court-approved visitation period, therefore, affords an offender the opportunity to carefully plan, assess, and conduct the crime without being suspected of parental child stealing until the court-approved visitation

Table 8-1
Precipitating Circumstances to Offense

Precipitating Circumstances	Number	Percent
Day visitation	11	12
Weekend visitation	30	33
Summer visitation	9	10
Separation prior to divorce	6	7
From babysitter's care	15	16
Denial of visitation rights	7	8
Physical force after argument	3	3
Child voluntarily left with offender	3	3
Other	7	8
Total	91	100

period has terminated. Offenders can easily camouflage their criminal intentions by employing a variety of approved circumstances to take control of the child.[1]

The Crime Site

The temporal aspects associated with parental child-stealing set a framework for the analysis of the modus operandi of the crime. The study of the location where the crime is committed might be valuable in untangling the circumstances surrounding the theft. The location of the crime may also be important in understanding the behavior of the participants. It might be possible to trace the flow of participants' behavior and, thereby, assemble a montage of events leading to the crime.

Examining the location of the crime could support or refute a number of conceptions regarding parental child-stealing. For instance, does child-stealing take place in public streets while the child is in progress to school? Is the child free of risk within his residence, or are children often abducted from their place of residence?

Analysis of the location of child-snatching utilizes the following categories: victim's residence; outdoors—streets or playgrounds; public facilities (such as shopping centers or government offices); victim's residence; offender's residence; relative's residence; school grounds—either indoors or from the play area; babysitter's or temporary care residence; friend or neighbor's residence; and "other" which included no information or lacked a clearly discernible location. These categories represent a classification as precise as possible because the investigation reports were generally clear and specific in noting the location of the crime. Only in a few instances did the location of the crime require extended searching that was often resolved by other documents within the prosecutor's file.

The most dangerous location for child-thefts is the victim's residence. The child's home was the location where abductions occurred in 67 percent (61) of the cases. The child's school was the second most popular location for thefts, as found in 12 percent (11) of the instances. Abductions from outdoors—streets or playgrounds—accounted for only 8 percent (7) of the crimes. This disproportionate number of crimes at the victim's residence further supports the perspective that snatchings are incorporated into court-approved visitation periods. Instead of an unannounced, bold theft from a public area, offenders may snatch children from their residences under the guise of visitation. Once in possession of the child, an offender can utilize the prescribed visitation period to transport and conceal the child. Table 8-2 presents the distribution for location of parental child-theft.

Why is the child's home the preferred location for parental thefts? In assessing the scene of parental child-snatchings, it becomes clear that offenders are seeking the most expeditious arena to take possession of the child. The location of child-thefts depicts those areas where a child's activities occur—home, school, and streets or playgrounds. Offenders can generally obtain physical possession of the child from his residence, but should a court decree or an uncooperative relationship exist between the ex-spouses, the child's school would be the most predictable arena to seize the child. And if the home or school is impractical to reach, the child has periods in transit on public streets that are often regular and solitary.

The next case describes a thirty-one-year-old mother's theft of five children aged seven to twelve years and indicates the ease by which possession of children was gained from the home of the victim:

On 2-10-78 the Susp., mother of the children, arrived at the home and was told she could take the children from the home but was to return them no later than 2200, 2-10-78. The Susp. did not return with the children. On 2-14-78 the Vict. received a phone call from the Susp. and was told that the children were O.K. and she was not going to return them. On 2-16-78 a second phone call was received. The Susp. told the Vict. she had returned

Table 8-2
Location of Parental Child-Stealing Offense

Location	Number	Percent
Victim's residence	61	67
School grounds	11	12
Outdoors/streets or playground	7	8
Public facility	5	6
Offender's residence	4	4
Relative's residence	2	2
Other location	1	1
Total	91	100

to Wash. State (home) and would not return. Certified copies of temporary custody order dated 2-10-78 giving custody to Vict. attached.

If the victim's home is unavailable for the abduction, the child can predictably be found at school. Child-thefts from school grounds appear uncomplicated since school personnel oversee large numbers of children and are reluctant to physically restrain an offending parent. The next two cases illustrate the attractiveness of schools as the location for a child-snatching. First, we have the theft of a four-year-old boy by his thirty-one-year-old father and an accomplice while the teacher was occupied with other students. The teacher's comments indicate her concern about a possible abduction. The report notes:

> On 4-13-78 I/O went to John Adams Nursery School in S.M. to inter. school personnel present w/offense committed. Teacher stated that on 4-12-78 at approx. 1115 hours a male adult known to her from prior contacts as Mr. Clark, father of Andrew came to the classroom where she was teaching a group of children which included Andrew. Susp. asked teacher if he could visit with son saying that his ex-wife had been telling him that son was sick and he wanted to see how son was. Teacher said "you're not taking him, are you?" and at that time a young, blond female had also come into the classroom and joined Susp. When teacher brought child up to them she heard Susp. ask child "Say hello to Henrietta. Teacher then became busy overseeing the other children while child was visiting with the two adults. After 5 or 10 minutes teacher took the other children to a patio just outside the classroom & shortly afterwards the schoolroom housekeeper came running out to her to inform her that son's father had taken him out of the classroom & was leaving the school grounds w/him. They both ran to the door but son, father & female disappeared.

In the second case, the offender boldly informed school personnel that the child was being taken from the jurisdiction. After an initial visit to the school during which he displayed passports, he returned three weeks later and removed the child from the play area while the child unsuccessfully screamed for assistance. The crime report describes this abduction of a five-year-old daughter by her thirty-four-year-old father:

> Ofcr met by school principal (Rio Vista School) Wit 2, who supplied below info. Wit 2—adv. ofcr that Vict's natural father (Susp.) had made several phone calls inquiring about Victs status in the abv. school. On 1-21-77 Susp. went to the above school & showed W-2 passports in his & Victs names so the school would release info concerning Vict.
>
> R stated she was divorced from Susp. in New York 2 years ago & has legal custody of Vict. R stated on 2-10-77 Vict. was attending Rio Vista School. R was notified to come to the abv. school, that a man fitting Susp. desc. had taken vict. from the school playground.

> W-1 stated on 2-10-77 approx. 015 hrs. her assist. obs. a M/W fitting Susp.
> desc. walking on the widewalk adjacent to the school looking in at the
> children. W-1 stated it appeared that Susp. was looking for his child. W-1
> later obs. Susp. at the school exit holding Vict. Wit. then heard Vict. cry
> out "help" & obs. Susp. running down the widewalk w/Vict. Wit. obs no
> vehicles.

If, however, the primary crime sites of the home or school are impractical,
the offender may choose to utilize the street areas necessary for transit between home and school. Although such thefts are rare, the case below
describes the theft of a six-year-old girl after she had left home for school
with a friend:

> Vict. stated that at approx. 0825 hrs. she sent her daughter, Subj, to school
> (Enadia Way Elem.) w/ wit #1 & wit #2 both 10 years of age. At approx.
> 1130 hrs. Vict. noticed that Subj. did not take her milk money to school
> with her so she (V) went to Enadia Way Elementary School. At the school
> she learned that her daughter had never arrived at the school. V then
> notified the Los Angeles Police Department.

> An Enadia Way Elm School ofcr. interviewed wit. #1 and wit #2. Wit #2
> stated that she and wit. #2 picked up Subj. at her residence then walked
> towards school with her. At the corner of Gault St. and Lena Ave. they
> obs. a silver color veh on the N/W corner. There was a man inside the veh.
> The man called out the window of the car "Jennifer, Jennifer." Subj.
> looked at the man (Susp) and stated "When did you get here?" The man
> (Susp) stated "I just pulled in." Jennifer then walked over to the veh and
> started talking to the Susp. The Susp then told us (wit #1 & 2) to go on to
> school. We then went on to school and Jennifer stayed talking with the
> man. I did not see her get in the car. I think she knew the man.

The locations selected for parental child-snatchings indicate that offenders desire a site that is predictable and affords ease of fleeing the crime
scene. The child's home, school, or transit patterns provide such an opportunity for offenders to seize their children.

Type of Force

The use of force during parental child-stealing crimes is rare. The analysis
of force used during the theft utilized two categories: only the threat of
force and the actual use of force upon either the custodial parent or the abducted child. In the 91 cases studied, 14 percent (13) involved the use of
physical force, while 8 percent (7) reported only the threat of force upon the
custodial parent or child.

Physical force in crimes of parental child-stealing is limited to the
degree necessary to secure possession of the child. In no case was a custodial

parent physically attacked during the process of an offender's taking the child. It must be recognized that an abductor's goal is to take possession of the child and flee the crime location. Excessive physical force would extend the crime period, perhaps draw others to the site should screams be heard, and intensify police investigations when a custodial parent displays serious physical injuries. The following case depicts one of the more severe uses of physical force in parental child-snatching. It is difficult to determine if the offender's primary intention was to assault his ex-spouse or to abduct the child which appears almost as an afterthought when the ex-wife flees. Physical assault between this thirty-year-old offender and his twenty-one-year-old ex-wife appear to have been established during their marriage. The case report involving the abduction of his four-year-old son states:

> Vict's ex-husband came to Vict's resid. on 6-1-78 & began kicking in door. Vict fled resid. via bedroom window fearing for her safety. (Vict divorce final on 5-9-78 & Vict states ex-husband beat her on prior occasions) Vict then called police from phone booth. Ofcrs. upon checking resid. discovered Susp. had taken Vict's oldest child. Vict showed ofcrs. divorce papers which included reasonable visitation rights on 1st & 3rd weekends & vacation periods. Vict. states Susp. has violated visitation rights by not returning children in past for two days. Vict. feels Susp. will flee to Puerto Rico (native country).

Parental child-thefts are, therefore, not characterized by physical assaults between participants. In the rare instances when physical force is a part of the snatching, it takes the form of restrained physical force sufficient to seize the child.

Witness Present

The theft of children by a noncustodial parent is not a solitary act. In 79 percent (72) of the cases studied, offenders took possession of children in the presence of a witness, usually the custodial parent. Only 21 percent (19) of the snatchings were found to be committed out of a witness's view. The trend to steal children in the presence of others should not be construed as a disregard by offenders in insuring the successful completion of the crime. The offense must be considered from the circumstances in which offenders must act. Young children are rarely left unattended by a parent or guardian. Also, for cases in which a visitation order is in effect, the visiting parent may take possession in the presence of the custodial parent. Although this is technically the initiation of the court-approved visitation period, it is, for all practical purposes, the guise under which the snatching is accomplished. Such general patterns of child care, therefore, should account for the unusually high number of child-thefts with a witness present.

Transportation Used by Offender

The type of transportation used by offenders during a child-theft can provide an insight into the sophistication of such crimes. Information regarding the offender's method of transportation from the crime scene was available for sixty-three of the ninety-one crimes. In almost every instance, that is, 92 percent (58), an automobile was the type of transportation utilized by child snatchers. The use of an airplane was reported in 6 percent (4) of the cases, while the offender ran from the crime scene in 2 percent (2) of the instances. Given the geographic design and lifestyle of the Los Angeles area, this finding appears axiomatic. It can be assumed that many of the twenty-eight cases for which no information is provided would also reflect the use of an automobile in transporting abducted children from the crime site. Also, in multiple-type transports—such as the use of an airplane—an automobile was most likely incorporated into the escape process. These factors would increase the already abundant use of automobiles in crimes of parental child-stealing.

Communication between Offender and Custodial Parent

Communication related to the child-snatching may be a particularly valuable factor in understanding the crime. The type of communication can indicate the subterranean intentions of offenders. An impersonal, nonresponse-seeking communique such as a letter or telegram may suggest that the offender's intent is only to let the custodial parent know who possesses the child. A telephone or in-person type of communication may seek to establish an exchange forum which can lead to analysis of the factors precipitating the theft or the deteriorating relationship between the parties. Communication, therefore, may possibly provide useful information concerning the motivational or interactive elements surrounding parental child-thefts.

As noted earlier, communication between offender and custodial parent following the crime affects the return or location of the abducted child. Of the 91 cases examined, 47 percent (43) involved some form of communication between offenders and custodial parents. In these forty-three cases, communication was by telephone in 72 percent (31) of the instances, by mail in 16 percent (7) of the cases, and in person for 12 percent (5) of the crimes.

Communication between participants of parental child-stealing takes three distinct forms. First, communiques may take the form of an announcement concerning the safety of a child and the offender's intention to retain the child. Such communications are usually short and by telephone.

The second type of communication in child-thefts is intended to use the abduction as a mechanism to influence the relationship between the custodial parent and the offender. These communications are always by telephone and clearly state the demand and that the child will be indefinitely retained. The third type of communication between custodial parents and offenders is in the form of rationalizing the crime. There was an extensive use of letters in these cases to convey an offender's intention to return the child when certain conditions, usually relating to the child's living environment, are changed. Communications to rationalize the child-theft frequently describe complex and long-standing problems that participants have failed to resolve. The following are excerpts taken from the police crime reports and illustrate the three types of communication between ex-spouses and in parental child-snatching.

Type 1, Announcements of Safety and Intention

The following telephone call was received by a custodial parent after her forty-year-old ex-husband had snatched her two daughters. The offender informed her of his acquiring the children and his intention of concealment. His final comment recognizes the difficulty authorities face in attempting to locate parental child-thieves:

> I've taken possession of the children and you won't be able to see them again. (When the R/P advised the Susp. that he could be charged with a criminal violation and taken to court he stated) They [the police] will have to find me first.

The next telephone call involves an offender's refusal to return his two sons, age seven and eleven years, following a court authorized weekend visitation in San Diego. The conversation is brief but thorough and states his intention of breaking contact with his ex-spouse. The telephone discussion states:

> Don't bother going to the airport. I'm not going to put the kids on the plane. We are leaving the State. So don't try to find us.

Type 2, Mechanism to Influence the Relationship

Child-theft, committed primarily to influence a reconciliation between the ex-spouses contain a coercive message. Such communiques emphasize the futility of attempting to locate the abducted child unless the offender's demands are fulfilled. Such a message is conveyed by the following telephone call made by a forty-one-year-old offender to his separated wife.

In addition to informing her that the child is being held hostage until she agrees to reconcile, the offender forcefully voices his disregard for the custody order. His announcement of the theft and its purpose are noted below:

> You will never find her. If you won't change your mind, it won't be us that suffers, it would be the family. [And during a second telephone call] I don't care if you have custody, you will never find her. I have her.

Type 3, Communication to Rationalize the Crime

An offender's communication to the custodial parent that is primarily a rationalization of the abduction appears rooted in a concern for the child's environment. These communiques are either succinct statements or take the form of extensive analyses of the child's suspected inadequate domestic situation. The following telephone call by a twenty-nine-year-old male offender after the snatching of his three-year-old son illustrates a clear yet brief communication:

> I am going to take my boy back to Ill. to live and you are not going to stop me. I don't want my boy raised in Los Angeles.

A second offense which includes communication by the offender to rationalize the crime is considerably different from the prior account. The offender, who is a forty-six-year-old policeman in Texas, discusses why he refused to return his eight-year-old daughter following summer visitation. His ex-wife was living with a man reportedly prone to violence. The child's grandmother notified the father of these violent episodes and he wrote the following letter to the investigating police agency. It carefully describes the suspected dangerous household and the offender's desire to comply with the custody decree if the child's home environment is safe. The letter reports the following concern by the offender:

> Letter to investigating officer at Glendale Police Department:
> Dear Sir,
> In regards to my daughter Linda, about three weeks ago my ex-wife's mother called me. She said that Nancy had moved in with a married man and that this guy had gotten angry with Nancy and beat her up pretty good. She also told me that he wrecked the furniture in the house and shot a hole through the bed, cut up pictures with a knife. To me it sounds like the guy is a little insane. Well, Francine advised me that I shouldn't send Linda back to Nancy until she leaves this guy as he may hurt her. Even if he didn't hurt her, if she were around to see a rampage like that it would do a lot of mental damage. The day this man Nancy is living with beat her, she notified the police. She called her mother and sister and they moved her out but a few days later she was right back in there again.

Nancy called me and asked when I was sending Linda home. I told her then what her mother had advised and that I wouldn't send her home until her mother thought it was safe for Linda to return. At first she was angry, saying her mother blew the story up. She said the man she was living with wasn't going to do it again. Well, anyway, she called a few hours later and agrees to let me keep her. She sent us Linda's birth certificate and shot card so we could put her in school and sent some more clothes. Well, now for some unknown reason she has decided to stir up trouble. If you could get in touch with her mother and her sister they could tell you a lot more than I can as I wasn't there. She works but is home after 5:30 pm I believe. I have tried to call Nancy but her phone has been disconnected and she only calls lately to scream and cuss up on the phone. When she is like this no one can talk to her. Well, I guess that about covers it. If you could call her mother she could fill in a lot better.

When I think Nancy is capable of caring for Linda I will send her back. Right now she just wants her back to spite me. I'm sorry she has caused you all so much trouble. When she gets like this she is insane herself, but that's another story.

P.S. If you could get child welfare to go over there and investigate to see if it is a fit home for my child to be raised in it would make me feel a hell of a lot better, or your own opinion in the matter. I am a policeman also and I know that people like the guy she is living with won't ever change, so what can I do? Linda loves her mother and I don't want to take her away permanently.

Communication between participants involved in a child-stealing case provides an insight into the offender's motives and concerns leading to the crime. It can depict the tangled relations and emotions that participants deal with. What must be recognized, however, is the fact that 53 percent (48) of the cases did not report any type of communication between offender and custodial parent. Noncommunication indicates an offender's callous determination to retain possession of the child and insure an undetected future that is free from interference by law enforcement or family. It can also be viewed as a weapon to inflict suffering upon the custodial parents beyond the child-theft itself. The loss of a child becomes increasingly painful without clear knowledge about the child's safety. Where can a search commence? Why was the snatching done? Without such information the custodial parent's attempt to locate an abducted child becomes nearly futile.

Relationship between Offender and Custodial Parent

Examining the relationship between the custodial parent and the offender can help trace the complex flow of events leading to the crime. The child-theft may be a continuation of an established climate of conflict between the custodial parent and offender. Is child stealing common for persons initiating a dissolution of marriage process, or does it occur between persons who have completed the divorce process? Are child-thefts the result of an unsuccessful attempt to repair a tumultuous relationship during a separation? Assessing the relationship between victims and offenders will clarify the tangled relations that spawn parental chlid-snatchings.

Analyses of the types of relationships between custodial parents and offenders revealed that 85 percent (77) of the cases involved ex-spouses. In only 14 percent (13) of the instances were the parties separated prior to a formal dissolution action, while 1 percent (1) reported a cohabitation relationship.

For most participants in parental child-stealing, relations are usually limited to arranging visitation or custody periods and resolving financial support obligations. But for certain others the interaction between parties is much more complex. Child-stealing can be the product of an environment in which the relations or contact between custodial parent and offender are strained or tenuous. In such cases the child-theft might signal the collapse of domestic relations between the parties. The following case of a thirty-four-year-old offender and thirty-year-old custodial parent illustrates the possible delicate domestic relations surrounding child-snatchings. Although the parents were divorced, they were living together at the time of the crime.

R/P advised me that for the past several months, she and her husband, now known as the Suspect, have been having family problems in that they are unable to get along and have been separated on and off for the past year. She advised that she had contacted her lawyer and had started divorce proceedings with the result attached to this report in the form of a Interlocutory Judgment of Dissolution of Marriage. U/S detective after reading this Order made by Judge Klein on 6-8-77 awarded the custody of the minor Victim #1 and Victim #2 with the mother (R/P) and with the Suspect having visitation rights which is depicted in the Court Order.

The R/P stated that she and her husband, also the Suspect, were attempting to bring the marriage back together ever since the Court Order and that they have been living together during this time but for the past month or so, her husband had lost all interest in the children and responsibility. She advised that he is unable to hold on to any job and has no desire in helping her with the payments that come due each month. She advised that they continuously fight in front of the children, therefore, she told the Suspect that she felt it necessary to recontact her lawyer to complete the divorce proceedings. She advised her husband that she was going to take the kids back to Mexico when the divorce was final for their own safety and that she would be leaving as soon as she was able to move out.

R/P states that on 9-10-77 approx. 9:00 am the Suspect told her that he was going to take the two victims sailing in Long Beach and that he would be back before long. She advised that approx. 6 to 8 hours after he left the residence he telephoned her and stated, "If you don't stop the divorce, you won't ever see your kids again". R/P advised it appeared that he was calling long distance as she could barely hear his voice and he also advised her that he was no longer in California. He further advised her that when she recontacted her lawyer and dropped the divorce proceedings, that he would send her money so that she could come and join him and his children.

For cases like the above, the abduction of children by a parent becomes the final mechanism in attempting to regenerate a deteriorating marital relationship. Such instances depict not the offender's desire to possess the child but a recognition that the marital relationship is severely ruptured. Child-stealing in such cases announces that should the marital relations be terminated the other party will be deprived of his or her children.

The embroiled relations between parties may continue to center on the domestic relations, not custody of the child, even after divorcce. An ex-spouse's close contact with a former spouse and extended family, and interest in and care of the children may foster a continued hope of a reconciliation. The following case describes the emotional nature of relations between ex-spouses and one individual's effort to reestablish a romantic liaison. The parties had been divorced nine months when the child-abduction occurred almost as an afterthought once the romantic offer had been refused. The twenty-three-year-old father's theft of his three-year-old daughter as her mother looked on is documented in the police crime report below:

> The Victim and Suspect were married for over a year, ending in a final divorce this year. The ex-husband (Suspect) has been living in California; however, until one month ago the Victim had been living with her two children in Illinois. During the past month the Victim has lived at the location with her mother, brother and sister, all of whom take care of the victim's two children, fathered by the Suspect. The victim and Suspect have been seeing each other frequently during the past and have been getting along fairly well. The Suspect has visited the children at the victim's house and on occasion has taken the children for the day with the victim's permission.

> Last night the Suspect was at the location visiting and just before he left invited his ex-wife to spend the night with him at the "Capri" motel. The victim refused the offer and the Suspect became enraged and left the house. Approx. three minutes later the Suspect returned, entering the house through the unlocked front door. The Suspect walked to the bedroom where Vicky, FN-2-1/2 wearing a green dress with a white collar, was sleeping. The victim ordered the Suspect out of the house, however, the suspect grabbed the child and began walking to the front door with Wit. #1 and #2 looking on. As the Suspect left he stated he wanted the other child and mentioned he might "blow his head off". The victim notified police who were unable to assist her at that time.

> On this date the victim responded to the police department with legal documents showing custody of the child. This report was initiated and

the following locations checked with no results. (Suspect's residence, & Capri motel, & friends residence). The divorce papers were placed into evidence and an outstanding traffic warrant was located for the Suspect. I received a late phone call from the victim who related that while she had been making the report to police the Suspect left a message at her house stating he was going to take a bus to San Francisco this evening.

Such snarled relations may account for the discovery that most parental child-snatchings are not immediately reported to law enforcement agencies. Child abductions were reported to authorities on the day of occurrence in 24 percent (22) of the cases and from one to seven days after the crime in 37 percent (34) of the instances. But a substantial number of crimes were reported extremely late to authorities—22 percent (20) between eight and thirty days and 17 percent (15) more than thirty-one days after the commission of the crime. The custodial parent's intimate knowledge of the offender, desire to insure the swift and safe return of the child, and perhaps compassion toward the ex-spouse may affect the speed with which custodial parents notify law enforcement agencies of such crimes.

For most participants of parental child-stealing, relations were usually limited to fulfilling the stipulations within the child custody order. But the relations between certain other participants indicate a complex web of subtle underpinnings that lead to the use of the snatched child as the ultimate mechanism used to force a reconciliation with an ex-spouse.

Multiple-Offender Crimes

Parental child-thefts are almost exclusively accomplished by a lone offender, as discovered in 92 percent (84) of the cases. In ony 8 percent (7) of the instances was the theft conducted by multiple offenders. White offenders were involved in 86 percent (6) and black offenders in 14 percent (1) of abductions by dual offenders. Of the seven multiple-offender crimes, 71 percent (5) were perpetrated by males and 29 percent (2) by female offenders. Frequently it was discovered that an offending parent's accomplice was a family member, perhaps a stepchild or sibling of the child to be snatched. The use of additional offenders appears to aid in assuring the young child that he or she is free of harm and in gaining his or her trust to enter the offender's vehicle. The trust and voluntary compliance of a child can eliminate the offender's need for physical force and insure an expedient flight from the crime location. In no case was a parental agent or vigilante used to complete the child theft. The following account by a six-year-old female describes how two offenders coaxed her companion into a vehicle. The trust and casualness with which the child approached the offender enhanced the implementation of the crime plan. The crime report notes:

Wit. 1 stated to R/O that while walking home from school, her and victim were stopped by a man in a red car. Witness stated to R/O that the only thing she could recall about the vehicle was that it had 2 doors. Wit. 1 stated that the man was wearing glasses. NFD by Wit. 1. Wit. 1. also stated to R/O that the girl in the back seat had long blond hair and was wearing a red top. NFD by Wit. 1.

Wit. 1 stated to R/O that when vehicle drove up, victim ran over to it and stated to the male driver "Hi daddy, where's mommy?" Wit. I stated to R/O the female in the back seat stated to victim "come here Christie." Wit. 1 then obsd. victim enter vehicle & wit in the back seat with the female/Susp #2. Vehicle then departed Westbound on Burbank from Reese.

Conflicting Custody Orders

Parental child-thefts are not the culmination of numerous legal attempts to gain control of the child. Rarely is a child abducted by a parent with a court order in conflict to that of the custodial parent. In only one instance was it discovered that a second, conflicting custody award was in force at the time of the crime. That lone case involved a forty-eight-year-old teacher and his ex-wife, each possessing separate court orders from two different California jurisdictions granting them custody of the seven-year-old son. The case report follows:

Ofcrs. were met at scene by Joyce Smith who stated that her ex-husband, Bill Smith, were legally divorced and that the Deft. (B. Smith) had kid-napped her son. Wit. Smith showed ofcrs. a court order dated Sept. 14, 1977 signed by Judge Jones in Dept. NWK, case # 6311. The court order listed Wit. Smith as a petitioner and awarded custody of Vict, minor child Tom Smith, to Wit. Smith. The court order listed Deft. as respondent and stated the respondent is restrained from removing the minor child (Vict) from the physical custody of the petitioner (Wit.) except upon prior express order of court or written agreement of the parties. The order further stated that the respondent (Deft) is restrained from removing the minor child from the state of California except upon prior express order of the court or written agreement of the parties. After showing the court order to ofcrs. Wit stated that the Deft and Vict. had been living in Spain since Sept. of 1977. Wit stated that the Deft had contacted her today 5-28-77 via telephone and that he and Vict. were staying at the Howard Johnson Hotel at Vineland & Aqua Vista in No. Hwd.

Ofcrs. verified with the hotel clerk that the Deft was registered in the hotel and was staying in RM 610. Knocked on the door and ID'd selves as police officers, Sgt. Jones at scene. Deft opened the door and verbally gave ofcrs permission to enter the RM. Ofcrs entered the RM and obs Vict. lying on the bed. Ofcrs informed Deft that they were conducting an investigation concerning poss child stealing. The Deft produced a court order for ofcrs dated Jan. 18, 1977 signed by Judge Mann listing Deft as respondent.

Defts court order stated: 1. respondent (Deft) is awarded temporary custody of the minor child subject to petitioners right of reasonable visitation. 2. petitioner (wit. 1) shall forthwith deliver physical custody of Vict to respondent. 3. both parties are restrained from removing the minor child from the county of L.A. without further court order or written consent of the other party. Deft stated to ofcrs that he and Vict had been living in Spain since Sept. 1977 and that he was teaching school. Deft further stated he knew he was to appear in court on Sept. 14, 1977 but failed to because his life had been threatened by one of Wits boyfriends. Vict voluntarily stated "where my dad & I used to live mommy would bring her boyfriends over and try to start fights and argue with daddy".

This clearly indicates that jurisdictional conflicts in determining child custody rarely induces parental child-stealing. The scarcity of conflicting custody orders does not support the view that child-thefts spring from an offender's frustration in securing possession of the child through conventional legal processes.

Note

1. Michael Agopian and Gretchen Anderson, "Characteristics of Parental Child Stealing Offenses," *Journal of Family Issues*, in press.

9 Conclusions and Recommendations

The purpose of this study was to investigate the nature and patterns of parental child-stealing—the abduction of a child by a parent in violation of a custody order. The analysis was based upon ninety-one cases of parental child-stealing reviewed for prosecution by the Los Angeles County District Attorney's Office between 1977 and 1978. The research studied three elements of parental child stealing. First, we examined the prosecution of parental child-stealing offenses. This included the filing of criminal charges, reason for rejection of prosecution, arrest of the suspect, amount of bail, extradition requests, case disposition, and sentencing. Second, we considered the participants of the crime—offender, custodial parent, and abducted child. Information about the participants included the age of offender and custodial parent, race, sex, marital status, and employment. The child's race, age, sex, and the location of the crime were also examined. Third, the situational elements and the modus operandi of the crime were analyzed. Items examined included the month of year, day of week, time of day of crime, and the time between divorce or custody and the abduction. The crime site, type of force used by offenders, presence of a witness, and type of transportation were also studied. Also included in this category were the communication between offender and custodial parent after the theft, relationship between the parties, precipitating circumstances prior to the snatching, multiple-offender offenses, and conflicting custody orders.

The following are among the findings from this investigation:

Slightly more than half of the parental child-stealing cases reviewed by the Los Angeles County District Attorney's Office were filed for prosecution. An analysis of the final case dispositions showed that 23 percent of the cases moved no further than the issuance of a bench warrant for the offender's arrest, while almost 20 percent of the cases were reduced to a misdemeanor.

The filing of charges in parental child-stealing cases is greatly influenced by which law enforcement agency investigates the crime. Slightly more than half of the cases from the Los Angeles County Sheriff's Department were so rejected. Referral to the city attorney for misdemeanor review or incomplete evidence each accounted for 32 percent of the cases rejected for prosecution.

In nearly 80 percent of the cases, offenders were not arrested or not in custody at the time of the crime investigation. Of those persons arrested, 82 percent received bail of five thousand dollars or less. Only about 20 percent included a request for extradition. Summary or formal probation accounted for 43 percent of the sentences for individuals convicted of parental child-stealing. A combination of jail and probation was imposed on nearly 40 percent of the convicted persons.

Nearly 70 percent of offenders and custodial parents are Caucasian. Males comprised 70 percent of the offenders. Both offenders and custodial parents are generally young. Most were between twenty-seven and thirty-one years of age. More than 70 percent of the offenders and custodial parents were thirty-six years old or younger.

In almost 65 percent of the instances a single child was snatched, while in 30 percent of the thefts two children were abducted. Caucasian children were snatched in almost 75 percent of the cases. Male and female children were abducted with equal frequency. Young children are the target of parental child thefts: 34 percent were three to five years of age, and 87 percent were eleven years old or younger. Only 47 percent of all children snatched were ultimately returned to their guardian parents.

Child-thefts are well distributed throughout all seasons of the year. They occur most frequently on the weekend. Friday, Saturday, and Sunday accounted for 53 percent of all child thefts. The most dangerous time period for snatchings is the late afternoon and early evening period between 2:00 p.m. and 8:00 p.m., which accounted for 43 percent of the Los Angeles crimes.

Parental child-stealing does not occur immediately after failure to gain legal custody of the child. There appears to be a planning stage or period of gaining the trust of the custodial parent during which the visitation parent adheres to the custody decree. Almost 40 percent of the thefts took place two years or more after a custody determination or divorce. Nearly 25 percent of the thefts occurred between six to twelve months following a custody award.

Nearly 70 percent of the child-snatchings occurred at the victim's residence. Physical force is rare during parental child-thefts, with only 14 percent of the cases involving some degree of physical force.

Almost half of the thefts included some form of communication between the offender and custodial parent. This communication took three forms: announcements of the child's safety and the intention of the offender; utilization of the snatching as a mechanism to influence the relationship between offender and custodial parent; or attempts to rationalize the abduction. In 85 percent of the thefts, offenders and custodial parents were ex-spouses, while 14 percent were separated pending a divorce action.

Parental child-thefts are rarely characterized by a surprise abduction from a public area. Most thefts, 33 percent, are perpetrated under the pretense of exercising weekend visitation. In 55 percent of the snatchings the offender gained possession of the child by invoking court approved visitation privileges. In over 90 percent of the instances the offender acted alone. In no case did a professional abductor snatch or participate in the criminal taking of a child. In only one instance was a conflicting custody decree in force at the time of the child-theft.

The dominant pattern of parental child-stealing that emerges from the present study suggests that the crime is carefully planned and spawned by the love and desire of a parent to maintain a full-time relationship with the child or to use the abduction as a mechanism to influence re-establishment of the ruptured marital relation.

Divorce is often a difficult and complex process for adults and children. Divorce does not erase the past nor does it create an unrelated future for the family members. Parental roles are greatly changed. A mother must recognize that she usually has a significantly changed role, the sole responsibility for parenting duties. She participates in the joys and disappointments of a child's development. In addition to these increased parental duties, a mother must adjust to life as a nonmarried individual. Her personal and family roles are considerably altered by divorce.

A father often must accept major changes in family roles and lifestyle. Generally, he will not be involved in the daily responsibilities of parenting. When a father's regular contact with a child is terminated, his authority and influence upon the child's development becomes indirect. A father must also adjust to a failure or loss by the noncustodial parent. With a custody order the visitation parent's time with a child is limited and may be carefully monitored by the guardian parent. The noncustodial parent may feel excluded from the overall duties of parenting—an appendage to the new single-parent family. Recognizing that legal custody of the child has been lost and that changes in parental guardianship by courts are rare, a parent may view child-snatching as the only option available to gain possession of the child. The extra legal nature of this activity may be rationalized by offending parents as motivated by deep and sincere love for the child.

This tug-of-love for possession of the child may develop over an extended period. A parent might be unsuccessful in various legal attempts to change an existing custody decree. A parent may believe that legal efforts to gain custody are biased, or a parent may initiate legal action for custody but quickly realize that the chances for acquiring the child are rare. The primary motivation that leads fathers to engage in child-stealing appears to be their deep love for their child.

An offending parent may also feel released from criminal and moral restraint by believing that a judge cannot adequately and equitably deduce the quality of a parent-child relationship. Such disregard for judicial decisions in child custody matters is not limited to offending parents. One judge has commented that "a judge agonizes more about reaching the right result in a contested custody issue than about any other type of decision he renders."[1] Child custody disputes can be viewed as the most perplexing and frustrating area of family law. A judge may more easily assess such factors as employment, residence, income, or lifestyle. Judicial ability to measure the emotional binding, love, and desire of a parent to share his life with a child is, however, very limited.

There may also be a strong undercurrent of belief by many individuals that family relations, and especially parent-child relations, are beyond the purview of criminal law. A judge's action in a divorce matter is a legal requiem that severs a marital relationship. Custody orders, however, may be viewed as an unfair obstruction of a loving parent-child relationship. Believing that such relations are sacred, a parent will more easily violate the custody order. In such instances offender's neutralize their criminal culpability and guilt by recognizing a parent's perceived fundamental right to possess his or her child. Offenders, therefore, believe that a judicial determination cannot interfere with their intangible parental privilege of maintaining full-time relationships with their children.

Offending parents may also be motivated to engage in child-stealing when a custodial parent is viewed as unfit or undeserving of the child. A variety of factors may be the basis for judging a parent unworthy of custody. Such factors might include diminished financial resources, lack of employment, frequent changes of residence, improper arrangements for the child's schooling or care, the parent's ability or desire to maintain sufficient contact with the child, or the custodial parent's maintaining a cohabitation relationship.

Another dimension of parental child-stealing from this study indicates that the crime is intended to aid in the reestablishment of the disjointed marital relationship between the offender and custodial parent. The abducted child becomes a mechanism which may be used to establish communication between the ex-spouses that was perhaps limited to arrangements for visitation or financial support. The theft of a child becomes a catalyst that influences a spouse to withdraw a divorce action or to bring about a reconciliation should they be separated prior to a divorce.

It is interesting to note that all cases which contained a plea by the offending parent to influence the relationship were by telephone. Such contact is the most direct yet safest method of communication. A personal appearance by the offender might be intercepted by the police, or a vital clue, perhaps an automobile license, might be discovered by the custodial parent. Although contact by mail is relatively safe, it is cumbersome for conveying sensitive feelings regarding the relationship. Such conversations were generally concise and explicit, with offenders clearly stating demands for a reconciliation or for withdrawal of divorce proceedings as necessary for the return of the child. The following call by a thirty-four-year-old offender to his twenty-nine-year-old ex-wife illustrates such an instance: "If you don't stop the divorce you won't ever see your kids again." Such demands are made with callous efficiency as acknowledged by the offender's reference to "your kids," not "our" kids. Since he had abducted both children, a five-year-old son and three-year-old daughter, it can be assumed that should his demands not be met his threat to disappear with the children would be actuated.

These instances illustrate the enormous emotional and physical traumas that can be created by the dissolution of families and child custody disputes. They portray parental child-stealing as symptomatic of more serious and continuing domestic disharmony between the offender and custodial parent. An offender may refuse to accept that a marriage is terminated, even after divorce. Possession of the child, therefore, becomes the ultimate weapon with which to induce a renewed attempt by the ex-spouses to reunite the family.

A general belief is that child-thefts are fostered by malice toward the ex-spouse. Embittered by an impending divorce or particularly caustic relations following a divorce, the offender might view parental child-snatching as a means of "getting even" with an ex-spouse. Custody in such instances is sought not out of a desire for the child but as a weapon of vengeance against the ex-spouse. The present study does not support the view that an offender's anger and vindictiveness toward an ex-spouse are the motivational elements in parental child-stealing. There were only two cases in which information was available to suggest that anger or a desire to inflict pain inspired the abduction. One case involved a thirty-four-year-old husband and thirty-two-year-old wife who were in the process of divorcing. Two sons, aged four and five years, were taken. The mother had a custody decree granting guardianship of the boys. On the evening of the crime she received the following telephone call from the offender: "I've got the boys and I'm gone. Now you can think about how I've been feeling. I'll be leaving with the boys for a thirty-five hour bus ride in a while. You aren't going to see them again." The conversation is chillingly efficient. It clearly announces that the children have been taken by the spouse, suggests that the custodial parent ponder the past trauma and suffering endured by the father, and informs her that they are breaking off communication with plans for concealment of the children.

A second case illustrates how parental child-stealing can be a powerful weapon used to inflict pain and suffering on a spouse. The following brief note, the only communique since the abduction, was received by a mother. It suggests that the abductor, a male parent, believes that she was to blame for the marital failure and dramatically states: 'I don't get mad. I just get even."

Animosity between ex-spouses involved in parental child stealing may actually be greater than discovered in the present study. Crime reports tend to be rather sketchy in regards to motivational information and are primarily concerned with establishing a modus operandi. A custodial parent might also be reluctant to inform law enforcement personnel of communication stressing vengeance as a motive because of fear that police will be suspicious or less zealous in pursuing the offending parent. Also, the motivations of the offender probably would not work their way into the official record, even though torture or punishment of the ex-spouse was the offender's goal.

Recommendations

Because parental child-stealing is a complex problem no one or two solutions will significantly impact this activity. Simply improving the law enforcement response to parental child-abductions, for instance, would be frustrated by continuing inequitable custody awards. In addition, solving the legal oversights which exclude offenders from prosecution would be impractical if law enforcement authorities were limited or ineffective. The following recommendations, therefore, provide an eclectic approach to reducing excessive relitigation of child custody determinations, providing a stable homelife for children while maximizing parents' contact with their children, and making for the effective enforcement of child custody orders. These recommendations are designed to remedy the legal and law enforcement loopholes that make parental child-stealing attractive to noncustodial parents.

Create Two Sets of Laws: One Making Parental
Child-Stealing a Federal Offense; and the Second,
Specifically Banning Such Activity in Individual
State Statutes

Currently, the Federal Bureau of Investigation does not have direct authority to intervene in parental child-abductions. A federal statute should provide the FBI with jurisdiction to investigate and assist in locating the missing child and offender. Presently, federal law enforcement assistance for parental child-stealing is limited to cases in which state charges are filed as a felony offense and an unlawful flight to avoid prosecution (UFAP) warrant for the offender's arrest has been obtained. The issuance of a UFAP warrant requires some evidence indicating that the offender has fled the prosecuting state as well as the concurrence of the United States attorney that such a warrant is necessary and feasible in apprehending the suspect. Such warrants become difficult to obtain in parental child-stealing cases. In many instances of child-theft, contact with the custodial parent is completely severed. Seeking to conceal their children's whereabouts, offending parents are discreet in camouflaging their lifestyles and identities. In addition, many offenders relocate into another community within the state in which the offense was committed. Without information supporting an offender's move across state borders, UFAP warrants are not issued for parental child-theft cases.

The recent adoption of the Parental Kidnaping Prevention Act of 1980 is the first federal statute designed to deter child-snatching.[2] In recognizing the often conflicting and inconsistent practices surrounding child custody awards, the legislation seeks to: promote cooperation between states to best determine custody of children, to deter interstate parental child-abductions, to facilitate enforcement of custody and visitation orders, and to induce and expand the exchange of information between states regarding children. The law becomes effective on July 1, 1981. Such a federal statute will provide a uniform national approach to assist custodial parents and local law enforcement agencies in upholding child custody orders.

The Parental Kidnaping Prevention Act of 1980 authorizes the FBI to assist and investigate parental child-thefts only in cases where a UFAP warrant is issued. It would also expand the scope of the federal parent locator service, which is now limited to searching for parents that are delinquent in child support payments, to aid in parental child-abduction cases. The act further provides that states give "full faith and credit" to child custody determinations. In an attempt to induce uniform standards for awarding custody, the legislation requires all states to adopt the basic principles specified by the Uniform Child Custody Jurisdiction Act.

The new Parental Kidnaping Prevention Act of 1980 does not create a federal crime of child-snatching. The original version of the bill which stipulated parental child-stealing as a federal misdemeanor was amended prior to enactment. This legislation, however, represents a major effort at the federal level to bring order to interstate child-custody disputes and adds an important deterrant to parental child-stealing. The impact of this legislation, however, cannot be fully gauged until its operation has been carefully assessed.

Individual states must also adopt specific statutes that make parental child-stealing a felony offense. The California legislation, for instance, provides prosecutors the discretion to file misdemeanor or felony charges. Such an option enables prosecutors to exercise discretion and a sensitivity to the uniqueness of cases when screening parental child-stealing offenses. State laws would allow local and state law enforcement agencies to coordinate efforts that will speed the recovery of children and the apprehension of offenders. Such laws would also enhance the possibility of extradition when an offender flees to another state. Both federal and state legislation is needed because offenders are presently able to circumvent prosecution by moving to "safe states." This dual set of statutes would close many loopholes that presently invite parental child-abductions.

In conjunction with the development of federal and state laws discussed above, interstate extradiction of offenders must be expeditiously granted. One of the most difficult aspects of enforcing a custody decree concerns locating the offending parent. In almost 25 percent of the Los Angeles cases prosecution did not move beyond the issuance of a warrant for the offender's arrest. It may be assumed that many of these instances involved interstate flight to avoid prosecution. When an offender is unavailable to authorities, the prosecution is frustrated, and the ability of offending parents to avoid criminal action by leaving the state may encourage future child thefts.

Relaxing extradition standards may also reduce further violence between the ex-spouses. If an offender and child are located in a state that will not approve extradition, the custodial parent might attempt to regain the child or confront the offender. Such violent episodes should be reduced if extradition is quickly granted and the offender returned to the proper jurisdiction for prosecution.

Increase the Use of Joint Custody Awards

In divorces, courts have traditionally divided equally all material possessions accumulated during marriage. But the most valuable part of a marriage, the child, is conventionally placed in the guardianship of one parent. This severely limits the noncustodial parent's contact with his or her child to "visitation." In these instances, mothers have almost always been awarded custody of the child. The awarding of custody to a single parent creates a wall around the child that frequently excludes one parent from contact and the responsibilities of parenting. Sole custody awards significantly limit a parent's access to his or her child. Such awards often create hostility between ex-spouses, subject the child to difficult loyalty conflicts, and nurture disrespect toward judicial decrees. Fathers especially come to view courts as noncompassionate enforcers of legal barriers between them and their children. Because noncustodial parents often perceive sole custody awards as inequitable, they may come to consider parental child-stealing as the most viable alternative to regaining their child.

Parents do not divorce children. The rights and duties of parenting continue beyond the dissolution of marriage. The increased use of joint custody awards supports a partnership in the duties of parenting, allows for continued contact witir the child, and induces amicable cooperation between the ex-spouses in creating a quality homelife for children. Expanding the use of joint custody awards would contribute enormously to the reduction of custody disputes. Sharing the responsibilities and process of parenting can lessen hostility between ex-spouses and provide for the continuing development of a wholesome parent-child relationship.

A new statute in California has recently been adopted in an attempt to increase the use of joint custody. It is based on the desire to preserve a child's equal access to both parents, and it encourages the sharing of parental responsibilities. The legislation should eliminate the "winner and loser" syndrome established by sole custody awards. The California legislation became operational on January 1, 1980 and states, in part:

(a) The Legislature finds and declares that it is the public policy of this state to assure minor children of frequent and continuing contact with both parents after the parents have separated or dissolved their marriage, and to encourage parents to share the rights and responsibilities of child rearing in order to effect this policy. . . .

(b) Custody should be awarded in the following order of preference according to the best interests of the child:

(1) To both parents jointly pursuant to Section. 4600.5 or to either parent. In making an order for custody to either parent, the court shall consider, among other factors, which parent is more likely to allow the child or children frequent and continuing contact with the noncustodial parent, and shall not prefer a parent as custodian because of that parent's sex.
The court, in its discretion, may require the parents to submit to the court a plan for the implementation of the custody order.[3]

The California law does not mandate joint custody awards or the co-parenting of children. It encourages parents to work together in creating a plan for sharing the rights and responsibilities of raising their children. This legislation is basically an expanded contact measure which affords both parents maximum contact, rights, and responsibilities in continuing the parent-child relationship following divorce.

The increased use of joint custody, however, poses a number of problems. It is impractical to divide a child's time in half because this creates instability. An effective joint custody agreement must distinguish between *legal* and *physical* control of the child. Specifying legal control of the child preserves the rights of a parent in decision making and access during periods when he or she is not in physical control of the child. Legal custody protects parental rights and privileges even when that parent does not have physical control over the child. Defining the form of physical custody should describe how a child's time will be shared with each parent. To insure stability in a child's homelife a joint custody decree can specify equal legal custody to both parents with physical custody to one parent. This reduces the "ping-pong" effect upon children who are shuffled from parent to parent primarily concerned that the number of parent-child contact hours be equal. Physical custody of the child might be divided on six-or-twelve month intervals. Joint custody awards which clearly distinguish legal and physical custody rights of parents insure the sharing of parental responsibilities while also stabilizing the child's homelife.

Logistical problems in the execution of joint custody awards can proliferate. Which parent is to make what kind of decisions regarding the child's school, religion, medical care, or vacation plans? Where are the children's possessions to be housed? Which parent will declare the child as an income tax deduction? An effective shared custody order should clarify such innumerable details to insure an orderly and positive parent-child relationship. These problems can be avoided by a detailed, written schedule delineating the rights and responsibilities for co-parenting.

Joint custody awards are not a panacea for child-custody conflicts. They may not be practical when parents exhibit great hostility or one parent is not desirous of sharing parental responsibilities. Joint custody awards require communication, amicability between ex-spouses, and the recognition that the best interests of the child must supersede the desires of one parent for total control of the child. By providing parents access to their children, joint custody should prove a valuable alternative to traditional custody decrees which have spawned parental child-stealing by disgruntled parents.

Establish International Treaties Specifically Addressing
Parental Child-Stealing and Child Custody Awards

The abduction of children across national boundaries is becoming an increasingly serious problem. Although numerical information on the frequency of international parental child thefts is very limited, the Office of Consular Affairs of the Department of State reports 269 such cases as of 1979. These cases include 125 in Europe and Canada, 44 in the Near East, 12 in Africa, and 2 cases in the Far East.[4]

The worldwide epidemic of divorce seems to have fueled international child-stealing. Most often, divorcing parents of different national origins are involved, and one parent takes the child to his or her country of origin. Also, international child-thefts may be prompted by the ease of travel and the growth of multinational corporations with employees situated throughout the world.[5]

Not only are offending parents able to circumvent criminal prosecution by interstate flight, but international flight also insures offenders safety from any criminal sanctions. A parent who abducts his or her child and flees the United States is immune from criminal prosecution. Parental child-thefts which involve flight across national borders are presently outside the purview of existing laws. The United States is not a member of any treaty that would facilitate cooperation from a foreign country to return a child to the custodial parent or an offender to the United States for prosecution of parental child-stealing. Conventional kidnaping is, however, included in existing international treaties and would mobilize law enforcement efforts for the return of an offender and child to the proper jurisdictional country.

In an attempt to deal with international parental child-thefts, a special commission of the Hague Conference on Private International Law has drafted a treaty titled "Preliminary Draft Convention on the Civil Aspects of International Child Abduction."[6] The agreement obligates participating nations to employ the most expeditious methods for the speedy return of children "wrongfully removed or restrained" within their country. The agreement concerns only children under sixteen years of age but applies to pre- and post-custody decree abductions. It would also include parental child-thefts when joint custody has been awarded. International violations of visitation rights are also addressed within the agreement. Foreign courts would have a limited role in such cases. They would not decide which parent should have custody of a child but only if there has been a wrongful abduction or detention. The Hague Preliminary Draft agreement attempts to accomplish on an international level what the Uniform Child Custody Jurisdiction Act provides at the national basis. The draft treaty continues under development, refinement, and review.

A comprehensive international treaty should provide for extradition in parental child-stealing cases and also promote cooperation between nations in recognizing and enforcing child custody decisions. Such a treaty might require entry of the jurisdiction issuing the original custody order onto the child's passport when he or she leaves the home country. A code number similar to the postal zip code could be utilized. A Children's Rights Bureau in the State Department could oversee such treaty stipulations.

Require Parents to Post a Security Bond with the Court

The everpresent danger of a child's being snatched can be extremely pernicious for custodial parents. And the determination of child custody is a complex, sensitive, and demanding process for courts. Because parental child-stealing is the blatant defiance of a judicial decree, the adherence to custody orders can be elicited through means other than criminal sanctions. Requiring a parent to post a security bond with the court as a requirement for exercising visitation privileges may prove an effective tool in enforcing custody orders. Such a bond could be secured in the form of financial or property assets.

The imposition of such a bond should be determined with extreme caution and wisdom by the court. It might be utilized only in those cases that can substantiate a clear threat by a parent to violate the primary conditions of custody established by the court. Such instances might include situations in which there has been a prior child-theft, the noncustodial parent has vigorously expressed his or her intention to secrete the child in violation of the custody provisions, visitation privileges require out of state or international transporting of the child, visitation is being allowed during the pendency of a prosecution for parental child-stealing, or in those custody disputes that are particularly volatile and a clear threat to the child's physical stability is established.

When a parent does not possess the means to post such a bond, his or her relatives might provide the necessary security. This would further reduce the probability of parental child-stealing. Relatives would be disinclined to aid in a crime scheme, and the parent's motivation to abide by the stipulations of the custody order would be strengthened.

Because this proposal links a parent's visitation privileges with his or her ability to provide a surety, courts must restrict the application of such measures to only those instances which display a serious predisposition toward parental child-stealing. Such an alternative will provide an additional assurance that parents will subscribe to the orders of a court in child custody determinations. It should discourage even the most committed parent from selecting parental child-snatching as a method of gaining possession of his or her child.

Provide Special Training to Judges Dealing with Child Custody Matters

Judges must make a commitment to design equitable and enlightened child custody orders. The delicate and emotional nature of awarding custody needs to be adroitly and carefully handled. When custody orders vary greatly, are decidedly biased, or are based on inadequate information, the probability of such an order being violated increases. Inequitable custody awards or determinations rooted in a flagrant abuse of judicial discretion will induce parental child-thefts.

Judges bear the challenge of providing parents with a custody determination that is isonomic. Such custody orders require creativity, skill, and perseverence. Educating judges with specialized training can aid them in drafting custody orders which are appropriate to the parties seeking custody. Custody awards must, for instance, move away from the biased tradition of almost automatically favoring the mother as custodial parent. Gender is an insidious basis for granting the responsibilities of parenting. With the increasing number of fathers desiring custody of their children, judges can no longer mechanically overlook fathers as the more suitable custodial parent.

To assist judges in preparing fair and workable custody arrangements special training in child custody matters should be established. Such programs need to emphasize the vast interdisciplinary information and resources available to judges dealing with child custody matters. They must also stress the array of alternatives and creative options available to aid judges in determining custody. The expanded use of behavioral scientists, negotiation betwen ex-spouses, and methods for developing thorough custody investigation reports would be of major importance to judges in resolving child custody disputes. Research and testing by social scientists, for instance, has become increasingly sophisticated and can provide valuable information and insights as a basis for judges determining custody. Promoting the negotiations of custody conditions between ex-spouses prior to a custody award should evoke increased compliance with an order. Custody investigation reports must provide judges with a thorough assessment of the circumstances and parties involved with the case. Judges need to demand more sophisticated investigation reports and place greater reliance upon such amalgamations of information when determining custody.

Special training programs might take the form of seminars and can be coordinated by the American Bar Association. Recognizing that judges dealing with child custody require a knowledge of responsive procedures and vast amounts of information to determine the proper course of custody, specialized training would avail them to decipher the complex underpinnings and innovative options which can prove helpful in creating just and functional custody awards.

A clear understanding of the Uniform Child Custody Jurisdiction Act by judges will provide uniformity in the application of this act. The act provides a valuable mechanism to bring order to child custody disputes but is not fully effective because of significant variations in the application and interpretation of its provisions. A standard national training program for judges should greatly increase the act's impact in settling child custody conflicts.

In addition to the principal recommendations noted above, a variety of secondary factors will impact the problem of parental child-stealing. The use of post-divorce counseling as a stipulation of the custody decree will improve the amicable interaction between ex-spouses and strengthen their commitment to responsible parenting. Such a counseling program can facilitate communication between the ex-spouses and also produce a coordinated parenting experience beneficial to the child. Far too frequently, hostility from a difficult divorce is sublimated and reappears in the form of a more serious problem, perhaps parental child-stealing. Post-divorce therapy will provide a vital resource for diverting or reducing hostility from divorce. Animosity from the divorce action may be rooted in the custody arrangement, financial settlement, or an ex-spouse's accusations of blame as to the failure of the marriage. This animosity must not interfere with the well being of the child. The demands and responsibilities of parenting continue after the dissolution of a marriage. Children of divorce must be provided sanctuary from the misdirected animosity between ex-spouses following divorce. The increased use of post-divorce counseling can be a valuable aid in reducing the antagonism following a particularly painful divorce.

The actual decision to award custody to a parent is not based upon any uniform standard. Criteria for granting custody are arbitrary and can vary widely from case to case. The welfare of the child is the court's primary concern. Generally, the most significant factors considered by a court in determining custody are: the ability of each parent to give the child love, guidance, and education; their mental and physical health; their capacities for providing the child with the necessities of life; the preference of the child; and the stability and continuity of the respective home environments. These factors are viewed as the primary legal basis for determining the best interests of the child. A uniform national standard for gauging the child's primary welfare would be enormously helpful in drafting effective custody decrees. A complex issue herein concerns how a uniform standard can be designed without restricting judicial discretion. Requiring states to subscribe to the provisions within the Uniform Child Custody Jurisdiction Act would be a significant improvement in the process of litigating child custody. A national standard utilized as a guideline for judges that also recognizes the uniqueness of specific circumstances and needs of the child would bring stability and uniformity to custody determinations.

The present study has discovered a number of characteristics and patterns surrounding parental child-stealing. It offers a view of the crime process, the offenders, and the victims involved in this unique activity. The information provides a clearer understanding of the interactive ingredients that make up parental child-abductions. It depicts the confusion between laws, the inordinate difficulty law enforcement faces in attempting to locate offenders and victims, and the limitations upon criminal prosecution for offenders.

Above all else, this approach sketches a portrait of the sensitive and stressful problem in human relations affecting many individuals after divorce. The restraints and sorrow parents create by child-snatching present a deep and continuing challenge to behavioral scientists. This study illuminates our understanding of this serious and painful repercussion of divorce.

Notes

1. See Alan Roth, "The Tender Years' Presumption in Child Custody Disputes," *Journal of Family Law* 15 (1976-77):423-462.

2. S. 105, 96th Cong., 1st sess. 1979. Also see U.S., Congress, *Hearing Before the Subcommittee on Child and Human Development: Parental Kidnaping,* 1979, 96th Cong., 1st sess., 1979; and U.S., Congress, *Joint Hearing Before the Subcommittee on Criminal Justice and the Subcommittee on Child and Human Development: Parental Kidnaping Prevention Act of 1979, S. 105,* 96th Cong., 2d sess., 1980.

3. Cal., Civ. Code, sec. 4600.

4. Brigitte Bodenheimer, "The Hague Draft Convention on International Child Abduction," *Family Law Quarterly* 14 (Summer 1980):99-120.

5. Georgia Dullea, "Parental Kidnaping: Boundaries Widen," *New York Times,* 29 January 1980, p. 14.

6. Bodenheimer, "The Hague Draft Convention," p. 99.

Appendix A:
Data Collection Form

Parental Child-Stealing

1. Case I.D. number (corresponds to D.A. _____

2. Card sequence number _____

3. Case filed or rejected by D.A.   Filed ____
                                                            Rejected ____

4. Why case rejected _____
5. Amount of bail ($) _____

6. Extradition requested or completed   No ____
                                                                Yes ____
                                                                No Infor. ____

7. If yes, from what state _____

8. Law enforcement agency reporting offense _____

9. Official offense charged   278 ____
                                             278.5 ____

10. Additional felony charged   No ____
                                               Yes ____

11. If above yes, what _____
                                   not applicable ____

12. Trial   No ____
                     Yes ____   Plea ____
                     No Infor. ____

13. Final disposition or last proceeding point _____

14. Sentence type _____

15. Sentence period _____

16. Offender's Race: Caucasian ____
                                   Black ____
                                   Mex. Amer. or Span. Surname ____
                                   Native American ____
                                   Other ____
                                   No Infor. ____

17. Age of offender   Mo: ____   Day: ____   Year: ____

18. Sex of offender   Male ____
                             Female ____

19. Marital status of offender _____

20. Occupation of offender _____
                                 No Infor. ____

Parental Child-Stealing *(continued)*

21. Income per month of offender _____

22. Arrested or in custody on present offense   No ____
     Yes ____
     No Infor. ____

23. Prior criminal history   No ____
     Yes ____
     No Infor. ____

24. Custodial parent's race   Caucasian ____
     Black ____
     Mex. Amer. or Span. Surname ____
     Native American ____
     Other ____
     No Infor. ____

25. Custodial parent's age   Mo: ____   Day: ____   Year: ____

26. Custodial parent's sex   Male ____
     Female ____

27. Occupation of custodial parent _____

28. Marital status of custodial parent _____

29. Race of child abducted   Caucasian ____
     Black ____
     Mex. Amer. or Span. Surname ____
     Native American ____
     Other ____
     No. Inform. ____

30. Child's age at abduction   Mo: ____   Day: ____   Year: ____

31. Child's sex   Male ____
     Female ____

32. Number of children taken in present offense ____

33. Abducted child by a previous marriage or relationship   No ____
     Yes ____
     No Infor. ____

34. Relationship between offender and custodial parent _____

35. Dissolution of marriage   No ____
     Yes ____
     Not Applicable ____

36. If above yes: Date _____
                           Location _____

37. Custody award at time of dissolution   No ____
                                              Yes ____
                                              No Infor. ____
                                              Other ____

38. Custody obtained since   No ____
                                Yes ____
                                No Infor. ____   Not Applicable ____

39. Custody awarded to   Custodial Parent ____
                            Joint ____
                            None ____
                            Other ____
                            No Infor. ____

40. Multiple custody decrees   No ____
                                  Yes ____

41. Any court order or warrant obtained against offender   No ____
                                                              Yes ____

42. Date of offense _____

43. Day of week _____

44. Month of year _____

45. Time of day _____

46. Alcohol present in offender or custodial parent during offense
              No ____   Yes, in both ____   Offender only ____
              No Infor. ____   Custodial parent only ____

47. Weapon used   No ____
                     Yes ____

48. If above yes, type of weapon _____

49. Who reported offense _____

50. Witnesses present   No ____
                           Yes ____

51. Multiple offenders   No ____
                            Yes ____

52. Any communication between custodial parent and offender after abduction
              No ____
              Yes ____
              No Infor. ____

Parental Child-Stealing *(continued)*

53. Physical force used   No ____
                                    Yes ____
                                    No Infor. ____

54. If yes, type _____

55. Location of offense   Outdoors or open space ____
                                    Public facility ____
                                    Custodial parent's residence ____
                                    Offender's residence ____
                                    Relative's residence ____
                                    School ____
                                    Other _____
                                    No Infor. ____

56. Precipitating circumstances to abduction:
        During weekend visit in accordance with decree ____
        During summer visit in accordance with decree ____
        During separation prior to divorce actions ____
        Taken from babysitter's care ____
        Taken by physical force from custodial parent ____
        Taken by physical force from temporary guardian other than
            parent ____
        Taken by threat of force to custodial parent ____
        Taken by untruth to temporary guardian other than custodial
            parent ____
        Victim voluntarily left child in temporary care of offender ____
        Spawned by denial of visitation rights ____
        Other _____
        _____

57. Child located or returned to proper guardian   No ____
                                                        Yes ____
                                                        No Infor. ____
                                                        Other ____

Appendix B:
The Uniform Child
Custody Jurisdiction
Act

.

The Uniform
Child Custody
Jurisdiction Act

TITLE 9. UNIFORM CHILD CUSTODY JURISDICTION ACT [NEW]

Title 9 was added by Stats.1973, c. 693, p. 1251, § 1.

OFFICIAL FORMS

Declaration under Uniform Custody of Minors Act, see Form set out following § 5158.

Law Review Commentaries
California legislation: Sources unlimited. Emil Steck, Jr. (1975) 6 Pacific L.J. 536.

Child snatching and custodial fights: case for Uniform Child Custody Jurisdiction Act. Henry H. Foster and Doris Jonas (1977) 28 Hast.L.J. 1011.

Evolution of California's child custody laws. Judge Everette M. Porter (1975) 7 Southwestern U.L.Rev. 1.

Prevention of child stealing. (1978) 11 Loyola L.Rev. (Calif.) 829.
Role of child's wishes in custody proceedings. (1973) 6 U.C.D.Law Rev. 332.

UNIFORM CHILD CUSTODY JURISDICTION ACT

Table of Jurisdictions Wherein Act Has Been Adopted

For text of Uniform Act, and variation notes and annotation materials for adopting jurisdictions, see Uniform Laws Annotated, Master Edition, Volume 9.

Jurisdiction	Statutory Citation
Alaska	AS 25.30.010 to 25.30.910.
Arizona	A.R.S. §§ 8–401 to 8–424.
California	West's Ann.Civil Code §§ 5150 to 5174.
Colorado	C.R.S. '73, 14–13–101 to 14–13–126.
Connecticut	C.G.S.A. §§ 46b–90 to 46b–114.
Delaware	13 Del.C. §§ 1901 to 1925.
Florida	West's F.S.A. §§ 61.1302 to 61.1348.
Hawaii	HRS §§ 583–1 to 583–26.
Idaho	I.C. §§ 5–1001 to 5–1025.
Illinois	S.H.A. ch. 40, §§ 2101 to 2126.
Indiana	IC 31–1–11.6–1 to 31–1–11.6–24.
Iowa	I.C.A. §§ 589A.1 to 589A.25.
Kansas	K.S.A. 38–1301 to 38–1326.
Louisiana	LSA–R.S. 13:1700 to 13:1724.
Maine	19 M.R.S.A. §§ 801 to 825.
Maryland	Code 1957, art. 16, §§ 184 to 207.
Michigan	M.C.L.A. §§ 600.651 to 600.673.
Minnesota	M.S.A. §§ 518A.01 to 518A.25.
Missouri	V.A.M.S. §§ 452.440 to 452.550.
Montana	R.C.M.1977, §§ 61–401 to 61–425.
Nevada	
New Jersey	N.J.S.A. 2A:34–28 to 2A:34–52.
New York	McKinney's Domestic Relations Law §§ 75–a to 75–z.
North Carolina	G.S. §§ 50A–1 to 50A–25.
North Dakota	NDCC 14–14–01 to 14–14–26.
Ohio	R.C. §§ 3109.21 to 3109.37.
Oregon	ORS 109.700 to 109.930.
Pennsylvania	11 P.S. §§ 2301 to 2325.
Rhode Island	Gen.Laws 1956, §§ 15–14–1 to 15–14–26.
Virginia	Code 1950, §§ 20–125 to 20–146.
Washington	RCWA 26.27.010 to 26.27.910.
Wisconsin	W.S.A. 822.01 to 822.25.
Wyoming	W.S.1977, §§ 20–5–101 to 20–5–125.

§ 5150. Purposes of act; construction of provisions

(1) The general purposes of this title are to:

(a) Avoid jurisdiction competition and conflict with courts of other states in matters of child custody which have in the past resulted in the shifting of children from state to state with harmful effects on their well-being.

(b) Promote cooperation with the courts of other states to the end that a custody decree is rendered in that state which can best decide the case in the interest of the child.

(c) Assure that litigation concerning the custody of a child take place ordinarily in the state with which the child and his family have the closest connection and where significant evidence concerning his care, protection, training, and personal relationships is most readily available, and that courts of this state decline the exercise of jurisdiction when the child and his family have a closer connection with another state.

(d) Discourage continuing controversies over child custody in the interest of greater stability of home environment and of secure family relationships for the child.

(e) Deter abductions and other unilateral removals of children undertaken to obtain custody awards.

(f) Avoid relitigation of custody decisions of other states in this state insofar as feasible.

(g) Facilitate the enforcement of custody decrees of other states.

(h) Promote and expand the exchange of information and other forms of mutual assistance between the courts of this state and those of other states concerned with the same child.

(i) To make uniform the law of those states which enact it.

(2) This title shall be construed to promote the general purposes stated in this section.

(Added by Stats.1973, c. 693, p. 1251, § 1.)

Section 2 of Stats.1973. c. 693. p. 1259, contained a severability clause.

Uniform Law: This section is similar to section 1 of the Uniform Child Custody Jurisdiction Act, see, 9 Uniform Laws Annotated, Master Edition.

Law Review Commentaries

Continuing importance of Ferreira v. Ferreira under Uniform Child Custody Jurisdiction Act. (1974) 62 C.L.R. 365.

Uniform Child Custody Jurisdiction Act; comment. (1974) 5 Pacific L.J. 365.

Library references

Infants ⚭18.

C.J.S. Infants §§ 5 et seq., 96, 99.

1. In general

Exclusive method of determining subject matter jurisdiction in custody cases in California is the Uniform Child Custody and Jurisdiction Act. which supersedes any contrary decisional and statutory laws. In re Marriage of Ben-Yehoshua (1979) 154 Cal.Rptr. 80, 91 C.A.3d 259.

Purpose of Uniform Child Custody Jurisdiction Act is to achieve greater stability of custody decrees and avoid forum shopping and, to that end, all petitions for modification are to be addressed to state which rendered original decree if that state has jurisdiction under the standards of the Act. In re Marriage of Schwander (1978) 145 Cal.Rptr. 325, 79 C.A.3d 1013.

§ 5151. Definitions

As used in this title:

(1) "Contestant" means a person, including a parent, who claims a right to custody or visitation rights with respect to a child;

(2) "Custody determination" means a court decision and court orders and instructions providing for the custody of a child, including visitation rights; it does not include a decision relating to child support or any other monetary obligation of any person.

(3) "Custody proceeding" includes proceedings in which a custody determination is one of several issues, such as an action for dissolution of marriage, or legal separation, and includes child neglect and dependency proceedings;

(4) "Decree" or "custody decree" means a custody determination contained in a judicial decree or order made in a custody proceeding, and includes an initial decree and a modification decree.

(5) "Home state" means the state in which the child immediately preceding the time involved lived with his parents, a parent, or a person acting as parent, for at least six consecutive months, and in the case of a child less than six months old the state in which the child lived from birth with any of the persons mentioned. Periods of temporary absence of any of the named persons are counted as part of the six-month or other period.

(6) "Initial decree" means the first custody decree concerning a particular child.

(7) "Modification decree" means a custody decree which modifies or replaces a prior decree, whether made by the court which rendered the prior decree or by another court.

(8) "Physical custody" means actual possession and control of a child.

(9) "Person acting as parent" means a person, other than a parent, who has physical custody of a child and who has either been awarded custody by the court or claims a right to custody.

(10) "State" means any state, territory, or possession of the United States, the Commonwealth of Puerto Rico, and the District of Columbia.

(Added by Stats.1973, c. 693, p. 1252, § 1.)

Uniform Law: This section is similar to section 2 of the Uniform Child Custody Jurisdiction Act, except that the words "dissolution of marriage or legal separation" were substituted for "divorce or separation" in subd. (3), see, 9 Uniform Laws Annotated, Master Edition.

Library references
Infants ☞19.1.
C.J.S. Infants § 8.
Words and Phrases (Perm.Ed.)

1. In general
Policy of § 5150 et seq. which dictates that issue of custody should be decided in court with greatest access to relevant evidence, required that request for change of custody made by father, whose right to relief was predicated upon his information and belief as to conditions in child's "home state" of Oregon, be stayed on conditions that father timely take appropriate proceedings in Oregon and that mother submit to jurisdiction there for determination of request for change of custody. Clark v. Superior Court In and For Mendocino County (App.1977) 140 Cal.Rptr. 709.

Visitation rights pursuant to stipulation modifying child custody provisions of prior dissolution of marriage decree were to be treated as "custody matters" under § 5150 et seq. Smith v. Superior Court of San Mateo County (1977) 137 Cal.Rptr. 348, 68 C.A. 457.

§ 5152. Jurisdiction; grounds

(1) A court of this state which is competent to decide child custody matters has jurisdiction to make a child custody determination by initial or modification decree if the conditions as set forth in any of the following paragraphs are met:

(a) This state (i) is the home state of the child at the time of commencement of the proceeding, or (ii) had been the child's home state within six months before commencement of the proceeding and the child is absent from this state because of his removal or retention by a person claiming his custody or for other reasons, and a parent or person acting as parent continues to live in this state.

(b) It is in the best interest of the child that a court of this state assume jurisdiction because (i) the child and his parents, or the child and at least one contestant, have a significant connection with this state, and (ii) there is available in this state substantial evidence concerning the child's present or future care, protection, training, and personal relationships.

(c) The child is physically present in this state and (i) the child has been abandoned or (ii) it is necessary in an emergency to protect the child because he has been subjected to or threatened with mistreatment or abuse or is otherwise neglected or dependent.

(d) (i) It appears that no other state would have jurisdiction under prerequisites substantially in accordance with paragraphs (a), (b), (c), or another state has declined to exercise jurisdiction on the ground that this state is the more appropriate forum to determine the custody of the child, and (ii) it is in the best interest of the child that this court assume jurisdiction.

(2) Except under paragraphs (c) and (d) of subdivision (1), physical presence in this state of the child, or of the child and one of the contestants, is not alone sufficient to confer jurisdiction on a court of this state to make a child custody determination.

(3) Physical presence of the child, while desirable, is not a prerequisite for jurisdiction to determine his custody.

(Added by Stats.1973, c. 693, p. 1253, § 1.)

Uniform Law: This section is similar to section 3 of the Uniform Child Custody Jurisdiction Act, except that the words "the conditions as set forth in any of the following paragraphs are met" were added to subd. (1), see, 9 Uniform Laws Annotated, Master Edition.

Law Review Commentaries
Continuing importance of Ferreira v. Ferreira under Uniform Child Custody Jurisdiction Act. (1974) 62 C.L.R. 365.

Library references
Infants ☞19.3(1).
C.J.S. Infants § 8.

United States Supreme Court
Acquiescence of parent to child's desire to live with other parent, jurisdiction of state of resident of other parent in that parent's action to establish foreign judgment, see Kulko v. Superior Court of California, etc., 1978, 98 S.Ct. 1690, 436 U.S. 149, 56 L.Ed.2d 185.

Index to Notes
In general 1
Construction with other statutes 2

Discretion of court 4
Home state 7
Inferences 3
Judicial error 6
Presumptions absent record 9
State of original custody determination 8
Stays 10
Waiver of objection 5

1. In general
Children, who were in California for two weeks when separation petition was filed and were there a total of approximately one month before interlocutory custody decree was issued in amended proceeding seeking dissolution of marriage, and who except for such time had lived in Israel their entire lives, did not have requisite significant relationship to California, and thus superior court did not have jurisdiction to pass upon issue of custody concerning children, whose only contact in California was presence of mother and maternal grandmother. In re Marriage of Ben-Yehoshua (1979) 154 Cal.Rptr. 80, 91 C.A.3d 259.

Where divorced mother who was resident of California failed to show that child's health or safety would be jeopardized if returned to his father in Rhode Island and where the record demonstrated that the father was able and willing to and in fact did provide a safe home and environment for the child who was entrusted to his custody under an existing court decree. California court was not entitled to issue even a temporary order changing the custody of the child, much less a permanent one; California court should have refrained from exercising its jurisdiction and should have stayed the proceedings to permit the final adjudication of the custody issue in the forum state of the nonresident parent. In re Marriage of Kern (1978) 150 Cal.Rptr. 860, 87 C.A.3d 402.

Mother who brought child to state in violation of foreign custody order in divorce case added nothing to her jurisdictional claim by asserting that California was better for child's health than Arkansas, from whence child was removed, and jurisdiction remained in state of Arkansas; claimed availability of evidence in California was also an insufficient basis for jurisdiction. Neal v. Superior Court of Los Angeles County (1978) 148 Cal.Rptr. 841, 84 C.A.3d 847.

Where when mother commenced Illinois proceeding for modification of custody provision of divorce decree, children had lived in Illinois with either their mother or father for at least six months, Illinois was "home state" of children and on that basis Illinois court had jurisdiction to modify custody order and change custody to mother, and thus California court, which awarded custody to mother and denied temporary custody to grandfather, was compelled to recognize and enforce that order. In re Marriage of Schwander (1978) 145 Cal.Rptr. 325, 79 C.A.3d 1013.

Evidence that parties lived in California during their marriage, that divorce proceeding and subsequent modification of child custody decree was heard and determined by California court, that the mother remained a resident of California after the divorce, that the children had visited with the mother in California, and that much of the evidence relative to the mother's fitness as custodial parent was in California sustained determination that California had jurisdiction under provisions of this section to consider mother's petition for change of custody even though the father had moved to Wyoming with the children following the divorce. Schlumpf v. Superior Court of Trinity County (1978) 145 Cal.Rptr. 190, 79 C.A.3d 892.

Although under § 5150 et seq. Oregon was the "home state" of minor daughter, custody of whom had been awarded to wife in California dissolution of marriage proceeding and who had lived with her mother in Oregon for more than six months prior to institution of custody and visitation rights modification proceeding in the California divorce court, the latter court had jurisdiction to modify custody and visitation proceedings and to hold mother in contempt for violation thereof, in view of findings that child and her family had equal or stronger ties with California as compared to Oregon and that child's interests would best be served by a California forum having optimum access to relevant evidence. Smith v. Superior Court of San Mateo County (1977) 137 Cal.Rptr. 348, 68 C.A.3d 457.

Where child was neither domiciled in state nor physically present in state, court did not have jurisdiction to adjudicate question of child custody. McDowell v. Orsini (App.1976) 127 Cal.Rptr. 285.

2. Construction with other statutes

Specific provisions of this section relating to jurisdiction in child custody matters prevail over conflicting and more general provision of § 4600 which provides that in any proceeding where there is at issue custody of a minor child, court may, during pendency of proceeding or at any time thereafter, make such order for custody of such child during his minority as may seem necessary or proper and provision of C.C.P. § 410.50 which provides that jurisdiction of court over parties and subject matter of an action continues throughout subsequent proceedings in action, as well as any express provisions in a custody decree which conflict with such specific provisions of Uniform Child Custody Jurisdiction Act. In re Marriage of Steiner (1979) 152 Cal. Rptr. 612, 89 C.A.3d 363.

Conflicting provisions of this section controlled over previously enacted C.C.P. § 410.50 of general application providing that jurisdiction over the parties and subject matter continues throughout subsequent proceedings in the action. Smith v. Superior Court of San Mateo County (1977) 137 Cal.Rptr. 348, 68 C.A.3d 457.

3. Inferences

In order to impose upon divorced father personal liability to support children, trial court, which had jurisdiction to determine custody of children, had to secure personal jurisdiction over nonresident father. Kulko v. Superior Court of City and County of San Francisco (1977) 138 Cal.Rptr. 586, 564 P.2d 353, 19 C.3d 514, reversed on other grounds 98 S.Ct. 1690, 436 U.S. 84, 56 L. Ed.2d 132, rehearing denied 98 S.Ct. 3127, 438 U.S. 908, 57 L.Ed.2d 1150.

Although former husband and the former wife, who presently resides in Oregon, could not confer on California divorce court jurisdiction that otherwise did not exist over subject matter of their dispute concerning child custody and visitation, from the parties' submission of visitation issue to the divorce court an inference could reasonably be drawn, for purposes of § 5150 et seq., that the parties considered the child's family and other ties with California to be stronger than her ties with Oregon. Smith v. Superior Court of San Mateo County (1977) 137 Cal.Rptr. 348, 68 C.A.3d 457.

4. Discretion of court

Where Illinois continued to be children's "home state" inasmuch as they were absent from that state only because their paternal grandfather and his wife had detained them in California, and the mother continued to live in Illinois, Illinois court retained jurisdiction to modify its order changing custody of children to mother from father and thus, in absence of showing that Illinois court would decline to modify its order and in view of lack of evidence of "emergency" justifying temporary custody order in grandparents while they litigated custody in Illinois courts, denial of paternal grandfather's request for temporary custody and award of custody to mother did not constitute abuse of discretion. In re Marriage of Schwander (1978) 145 Cal.Rptr. 325, 79 C.A.3d 1013.

In view of possibility of concurrent jurisdiction of California and Oregon courts to determine father's request for order changing custody of child and fact that Oregon was state with which child and her family had closest connection, in which significant evidence concerning her care, protection, training and personal relationship was most readily available and in which she had made her home with her mother for over five years, failure to stay local proceedings on conditions that father timely take appropriate proceedings in Oregon and that mother submit to jurisdiction there for determination of change of custody request was abuse of discretion. Clark v. Superior Court In and For Mendocino County (1977) 140 Cal.Rptr. 709, 73 C.A.3d 298.

5. Waiver of objection

Husband did not waive his right to challenge jurisdiction of California court under this section by waiting to raise the issue until after he had made his appearance; that objection is not waived by the failure to raise it at the earliest possible time. Schlumpf v. Superior Court of Trinity County (1978) 145 Cal.Rptr. 190, 79 C.A.3d 892.

6. Judicial error

Even if Colorado court did not correctly apply or follow provision of Uniform Child Custody Jurisdiction Act as to pending child custody proceeding in California or Colorado statute as to California still having jurisdiction, such statutes by their terms assumed jurisdiction otherwise present, and thus a violation of such statutes rose only to level of judicial error within Colorado court's fundamental jurisdiction, and, since Colorado custody modification decree, which modified prior California custody decree, was final, such nonjurisdictional error did not subject Colorado decree to collateral attack. In re Marriage of Steiner (1979) 152 Cal.Rptr. 612, 89 C.A.3d 363.

7. Home state

Where, while wife and minor child were residing in Colorado at time petition for dissolution was filed in California in November 1974, wife was in California for dissolution hearing in February 1975 and for some of other proceedings in spring of 1975, wife and minor child returned to Colorado on May 6, 1975, and wife commenced a modification proceeding in Colorado on October 28, 1975, 175 days later, Colorado was not home state under provision of Uniform Child Custody Jurisdiction Act setting forth bases for exercise of jurisdiction by Colorado courts in child custody matters, since child had not resided there continuously for six consecutive months immediately preceding filing of petition in Colorado. In re Marriage of Steiner (1979) 152 Cal.Rptr. 612, 89 C.A.3d 363.

8. State of original custody determination

A state should not assume authority to modify a custody decree solely upon fact that it was state that initially made custody determination since such would ignore significant relationship test basis of acquiring jurisdiction to modify a decree and since such would ignore central concept that it is best interest of child that governs and not interest or desires of wrangling parents. In re Marriage of Steiner (1979) 152 Cal.Rptr. 612, 89 C.A.3d 363.

9. Presumptions absent record

In light of husband's failure to supply court with a record of Colorado proceeding, it had to be presumed in support of Colorado custody modification decree, which, by awarding custody to wife, modified prior California custody decree alternating custody between husband and wife, that Colorado court followed law and made determination, adverse to husband that, at time it entertained wife's petition to modify California custody decree, California was neither home state nor met significant relationship test. In re Marriage of Steiner (1979) 152 Cal.Rptr. 612, 89 C.A.3d 363.

10. Stays

Child custody proceeding instituted by mother to establish a North Dakota divorce decree giving her custody of parties' minor son was subject to being stayed on request of father for prohibition during pendency of hearings concerning son's custody currently being conducted in North Dakota courts where custody proceeding was pending in North Dakota and relief sought amounted to a modification of a North Dakota decree when that state still had jurisdiction and had assumed it. Palm v. Superior Court (App.1979) 158 Cal.Rptr. 786.

§ 5153. Notice and opportunity to be heard

Before making a decree under this title, reasonable notice and opportunity to be heard shall be given to the contestants, any parent whose parental rights have not been previously terminated, and any person who has physical custody of the child. If any of these persons is outside this state, notice and opportunity to be heard shall be given pursuant to Section 5154.
(Added by Stats.1973, c. 693, p. 1253, § 1.)

Uniform Law: This section is similar to section 4 of the Uniform Child Custody Jurisdiction Act, see, 9 Uniform Laws Annotated, Master Edition.

Library references
Infants ⚏19.3(3).
C.J.S. Infants § 8.

1. In general

Before entering order with respect to father's visitation rights with child in custody of mother, mother was entitled to notice and opportunity to be heard. McDowell v. Orsini (App.1976) 127 Cal.Rptr. 285.

§ 5154. Notice to persons outside this state; submission to jurisdiction

(1) Notice required for the exercise of jurisdiction over a person outside this state shall be given in a manner reasonably calculated to give actual notice, and may be made in any of the following ways:

(a) By personal delivery outside this state in the manner prescribed for service of process within this state.

(b) In the manner prescribed by the law of the place in which the service is made for service of process in that place in an action in any of its courts of general jurisdiction.

(c) By any form of mail addressed to the person to be served and requesting a receipt.

(d) As directed by the court (including publication, if other means of notification are ineffective).

(2) Notice under this section shall be served, mailed, delivered, or last published at least 10 days before any hearing in this state.

(3) Proof of service outside this state may be made by affidavit of the individual who made the service, or in the manner prescribed by the law of this state, the order pursuant to which the service is made, or the law of the place in which the service is made. If service is made by mail, proof may be a receipt signed by the addressee or other evidence of delivery to the addressee.

(4) Notice is not required if a person submits to the jurisdiction of the court. (Added by Stats.1973, c. 693, p. 1253, § 1.)

Uniform Law: This section is similar to section 5 of the Uniform Child Custody Jurisdiction Act, except that the words "made in any of the following ways" were added in subd. (1) and "10" days notice was specified in (d)(2), see. 9 Uniform Laws Annotated, Master Edition.

Library references
Infants ⚭19.3(3).
C.J.S. Infants § 8.

§ 5155. Simultaneous proceedings in other states

(1) A court of this state shall not exercise its jurisdiction under this title if at the time of filing the petition a proceeding concerning the custody of the child was pending in a court of another state exercising jurisdiction substantially in conformity with this title, unless the proceeding is stayed by the court of the other state because this state is a more appropriate forum or for other reasons.

(2) Before hearing the petition in a custody proceeding the court shall examine the pleadings and other information supplied by the parties under 5159 and shall consult the child custody registry established under 5163 concerning the pendency of proceedings with respect to the child in other states. If the court has reason to believe that proceedings may be pending in another state it shall direct an inquiry to the state court administrator or other appropriate official of the other state.

(3) If the court is informed during the course of the proceeding that a proceeding concerning the custody of the child was pending in another state before the court assumed jurisdiction it shall stay the proceeding and communicate with the court in which the other proceeding is pending to the end that the issue may be litigated in the more appropriate forum and that information be exchanged in accordance with Sections 5168 through 5171. If a court of this state has made a custody decree before being informed of a pending proceeding in a court of another state it shall immediately inform that court of the fact. If the court is informed that a proceeding was commenced in another state after it assumed jurisdiction it shall likewise inform the other court to the end that the issues may be litigated in the more appropriate forum. (Added by Stats.1973, c. 693, p. 1254, § 1.)

Nonexistence of state-mandated local costs, see note under § 5150.
Uniform Law: This section is similar to section 6 of the Uniform Child Custody Jurisdiction Act, see. 9 Uniform Laws Annotated, Master Edition.
Law Review Commentaries
Continuing importance of Ferreira v. Ferreira under Uniform Child Custody Jurisdiction Act. (1974) 62 C.L.R. 365.
Library references
Infants ⚭18.
C.J.S. Infants §§ 5 et seq., 96, 99.

Index to Notes

In general 1
Stay of proceeding 2

------

1. In general
Colorado version of this section of Uniform Child Custody Jurisdiction Act which provides that a Colorado court shall not exercise its jurisdiction if a proceeding concerning custody of child is pending in another state, did not bar Colorado court from taking jurisdiction, because custody proceeding was not pending in California, since continuing jurisdiction of California court under § 4600 and C.C.P. § 410.50 could not under the act be deemed to be a proceeding pending within meaning of Colorado statute; moreover, fact that California child custody order was appealable and time for appeal expired before proceeding in Colorado was commenced meant that, by definition under C.C.P. § 1049, proceeding was not then pending in California. In re Marriage of Steiner (1979) 152 Cal.Rptr. 612, 89 C.A.3d 363.

2. Stay of proceeding
Child custody proceeding instituted by mother to establish a North Dakota divorce decree giving her custody of parties' minor son was subject to being stayed on request of father for prohibition during pendency of hearings concerning son's custody currently being conducted in North Dakota courts where custody proceeding was pending in North Dakota and relief sought amounted to a modification of a North Dakota decree when that state still had jurisdiction and had assumed it. Palm v. Superior Court (App.1979) 158 Cal.Rptr. 786.

§ 5156. Inconvenient forum

(1) A court which has jurisdiction under this title to make an initial or modification decree may decline to exercise its jurisdiction any time before making

a decree if it finds that it is an inconvenient forum to make a custody determination under the circumstances of the case and that a court of another state is a more appropriate forum.

(2) A finding of inconvenient forum may be made upon the court's own motion or upon motion of a party or a guardian ad litem or other representative of the child.

(3) In determining if it is an inconvenient forum, the court shall consider if it is in the interest of the child that another state assume jurisdiction. For this purpose it may take into account the following factors, among others:

(a) If another state is or recently was the child's home state.

(b) If another state has a closer connection with the child and his family or with the child and one or more of the contestants.

(c) If substantial evidence concerning the child's present or future care, protection, training, and personal relationships is more readily available in another state.

(d) If the parties have agreed on another forum which is no less appropriate.

(e) If the exercise of jurisdiction by a court of this state would contravene any of the purposes stated in Section 5150.

(4) Before determining whether to decline or retain jurisdiction the court may communicate with a court of another state and exchange information pertinent to the assumption of jurisdiction by either court with a view to assuring that jurisdiction will be exercised by the more appropriate court and that a forum will be available to the parties.

(5) If the court finds that it is an inconvenient forum and that a court of another state is a more appropriate forum, it may dismiss the proceedings, or it may stay the proceedings upon condition that a custody proceeding be promptly commenced in another named state or upon any other conditions which may be just and proper, including the condition that a moving party stipulate his consent and submission to the jurisdiction of the other forum.

(6) The court may decline to exercise its jurisdiction under this title if a custody determination is incidental to an action for divorce or another proceeding while retaining jurisdiction over the divorce or other proceeding.

(7) If it appears to the court that it is clearly an inappropriate forum it may require the party who commenced the proceedings to pay, in addition to the costs of the proceedings in this state, necessary travel and other expenses, including attorney's fees, incurred by other parties or their witnesses. Payment is to be made to the clerk of the court for remittance to the proper party.

(8) Upon dismissal or stay of proceedings under this section the court shall inform the court found to be the more appropriate forum of this fact, or if the court which would have jurisdiction in the other state is not certainly known, shall transmit the information to the court administrator or other appropriate official for forwarding to the appropriate court.

(9) Any communication received from another state informing this state of a finding of inconvenient forum because a court of this state is the more appropriate forum shall be filed in the custody registry of the appropriate court. Upon assuming jurisdiction the court of this state shall inform the original court of this fact.

(Added by Stats.1973, c. 693, p. 1254, § 1.)

Uniform Law: This section is similar to section 7 of the Uniform Child Custody Jurisdiction Act. see, 9 Uniform Laws Annotated. Master Edition.

Law Review Commentaries

Continuing importance of Ferreira v. Ferreira under Uniform Child Custody Jurisdiction Act. (1974) 62 C.L.R. 365.

Library references

Infants ⊂⊃18.
C.J.S. Infants §§ 5 et seq., 96, 99.

Index to Notes

1. In general

This section does not give a court authority to determine if it has a superior right to proceed where another court is also asserting jurisdiction, but provides a means to resolve issue in an orderly manner without letting a state make factual rulings binding on another. Palm v. Superior Court (App.1979) 158 Cal.Rptr. 786.

Court which has jurisdiction to make an initial or modification custody decree may decline to exercise its jurisdiction any time before making a decree if it finds that it is an inconvenient forum to make a custody determination under the circumstances of the case and that a court of another state is a more appropriate forum. Bosse v. Superior Court for Santa Clara County (1979) 152 Cal.Rptr. 665, 89 C.A.3d 440.

Where Montana had been the child's home state for the past 2½ years, where Montana had a closer connection with the child and the mother than did California with the child and the father, where evidence concerning the child's present or future care, protection, training, and personal relationships was more readily available in Montana, and where the exercise of jurisdiction by California court could contravene the general purposes of the Uniform Child Custody Jurisdiction Act, California court should exercise its discretion to issue a stay of proceedings in California to permit final adjudication in Montana of the issue of custody unless the mother's unclean hands, permitted the California court to refrain jurisdiction. Id.

Where children were living in Wyoming with their father and his second wife with whom they had resided for nine years, where the children had lived in Wyoming for five years, where the children had obtained schooling and education in Wyoming, and where evidence of the relationship and the children's education and the effect that a change would have on the children was most readily available at the site of the children's home in Wyoming, California courts, which had jurisdiction under § 5152 should defer to the courts of Wyoming, which also had jurisdiction, even though evidence of the mother's suitability as a custodial parent was in California. Schlumpf v. Superior Court of Trinity County (1978) 145 Cal.Rptr. 190, 79 C.A.3d 892.

Policy of § 5150 et seq. which dictates that issue of custody should be decided in court with greatest access to relevant evidence, required that request for change of custody made by father, whose right to relief was predicated upon his information and belief as to conditions in child's "home state" of Oregon, be stayed on conditions that father timely take appropriate proceedings in Oregon and that mother submit to jurisdiction there for determination of

request for change of custody. Clark v. Superior Court in and For Mendocino County (1977) 140 Cal.Rptr. 709, 73 C.A. 3d 298.

In view of possibility of concurrent jurisdiction of California and Oregon courts to determine father's request for order changing custody of child and fact that Oregon was state with which child and her family had closest connection, in which significant evidence concerning her care, protection, training and personal relationship was most readily available and in which she had made her home with her mother for over five years, failure to stay local proceedings on conditions that father timely take appropriate proceedings in Oregon and that mother submit to jurisdiction there for determination of change of custody request was abuse of discretion. Id.

1.5 Priority of courts

Under this section, state which enjoys priority of time in initiating proceedings will proceed if dispute is not resolved by agreement or consent of other court. Palm v. Superior Court (App.1979) 158 Cal.Rptr. 786.

2. Stays

Allegations that mother, who was living in Montana with the child, had violated provisions of custody decree by declining to allow the father to exercise his visitation rights did not show such unclean hands on the part of the mother as to allow California courts to retain jurisdiction over the issue of custody and it was thus an abuse of discretion for California trial court not to stay proceedings brought in California pending the outcome of custody proceedings, pending in Montana. Bosse v. Superior Court for Santa Clara County (1979) 152 Cal.Rptr. 665, 89 C.A.3d 440.

The court's discretion to deny a stay in an interstate custody case must be narrowly exercised in order to avoid encouragement of unlawful abduction and retention of children. In re Marriage of Kern (1978) 150 Cal.Rptr. 860, 87 C.A.3d 402.

3. Clean hands doctrine

In child custody proceeding, as in guardianship and adoption proceedings, question of clean hands should be subordinated to the court's primary consideration in child custody matters as expressed in the Uniform Child Custody Jurisdiction Act, i. e., whether, under the circumstances of the case, the action taken by the court is in the interest of the child. Bosse v. Superior Court for Santa Clara County (1979) 152 Cal.Rptr. 665, 89 C.A.3d 440.

§ 5157. Jurisdiction declined by reason of conduct

(1) If the petitioner for an initial decree has wrongfully taken the child from another state or has engaged in similar reprehensible conduct the court may decline to exercise jurisdiction for purposes of adjudication of custody if this is just and proper under the circumstances.

(2) Unless required in the interest of the child, the court shall not exercise its jurisdiction to modify a custody decree of another state if the petitioner, without consent of the person entitled to custody has improperly removed the child from the physical custody of the person entitled to custody or has improperly retained the child after a visit or other temporary relinquishment of physical custody. If the petitioner has violated any other provision of a custody decree of another state the court may decline to exercise its jurisdiction if this is just and proper under the circumstances.

(3) Where the court declines to exercise jurisdiction upon petition for an initial custody decree pursuant to subdivision (1), the court shall notify the parent or other appropriate person and the prosecuting attorney of the appropriate jurisdiction in the other state. If a request to that effect is received from the other state,

Underline indicates changes or additions by amendment

the court shall order the petitioner to appear with the child in a custody proceeding instituted in the other state in accordance with Section 5169. If no such request is made within a reasonable time after such notification, the court may entertain a petition to determine custody by the petitioner if it has jurisdiction pursuant to Section 5152.

(4) Where the court refuses to assume jurisdiction to modify the custody decree of another state pursuant to subdivision (2) or pursuant to Section 5163, the court shall notify the person who has legal custody under the decree of the other state and the prosecuting attorney of the appropriate jurisdiction in the other state and may order the petitioner to return the child to the person who has legal custody. If it appears that the order will be ineffective and the legal custodian is ready to receive the child within a period of a few days, the court may place the child in a foster care home for such period, pending return of the child to the legal custodian. At the same time, the court shall advise the petitioner that any petition for modification of custody must be directed to the appropriate court of the other state which has continuing jurisdiction, or, in the event that that court declines jurisdiction, to a court in a state which has jurisdiction pursuant to Section 5152.

(5) In appropriate cases a court dismissing a petition under this section may charge the petitioner with necessary travel and other expenses, including attorney's fees * * * and the cost of returning the child to another state.

(Added by Stats.1973, c. 693, p. 1255, § 1. Amended by Stats.1976, c. 1399, p. 6313, § 5.)

1976 Amendment. Inserted subds. (3) and (4); renumbered former subd. (3) as (5); and substituted at the end thereof, "and the cost of returning the child to another state" for ", incurred by other parties or their witnesses".

Uniform Laws: This section is similar to section 8 of the Uniform Child Custody Jurisdiction Act, see, 9 Uniform Laws Annotated, Master Edition.

Law Review Commentaries
Continuing importance of Ferreira v. Ferreira under Uniform Child Custody Jurisdiction Act. (1974) 62 C.L.R. 365.

Library references
Infants ⊂⇒18.
C.J.S. Infants §§ 5 et seq., 96, 99.

1. In general
Husband, who without wife's consent had surreptitiously removed children and taken them to Israel after being enjoined not to remove children from jurisdiction of the court, was not barred from contesting validity of California custody decree under doctrine of unclean hands, which cannot be basis for subject matter jurisdiction, which has only been applied against wrongdoing parent who sought to invoke jurisdiction of California court and who was in clear violation of another state's decree, and application of which is discretionary. In re Marriage of Ben-Yehoshua (1979) 154 Cal. Rptr. 80, 91 C.A.3d 259.

§ 5158. Information under oath to be submitted to court

(1) Every party in a custody proceeding in his first pleading or in an affidavit attached to that pleading shall give information under oath as to the child's present address, the places where the child has lived within the last five years, and the names and present addresses of the persons with whom the child has lived during that period. In this pleading or affidavit every party shall further declare under oath as to each of the following whether:

(a) He has participated, as a party, witness, or in any other capacity, in any other litigation concerning the custody of the same child in this or any other state.

(b) He has information of any custody proceeding concerning the child pending in a court of this or any other state.

(c) He knows of any person not a party to the proceedings who has physical custody of the child or claims to have custody or visitation rights with respect to the child.

(2) If the declaration as to any of the above items is in the affirmative the declarant shall give additional information under oath as required by the court. The court may examine the parties under oath as to details of the information furnished and as to other matters pertinent to the court's jurisdiction and the disposition of the case.

(3) Each party has a continuing duty to inform the court of any custody proceeding concerning the child in this or any other state of which he obtained information during this proceeding.

(Added by Stats.1973, c. 693, p. 1256, § 1.)

Asterisks * * * Indicate deletions by amendment

CIVIL CODE

OFFICIAL FORMS

Name, Address and Telephone No. of Attorney(s)

Space Below for Use of Court Clerk Only

Attorney(s) for

SUPERIOR COURT OF CALIFORNIA, COUNTY OF . . . .

In re the marriage of

Petitioner

and

Respondent

CASE NUMBER

DECLARATION UNDER
UNIFORM CUSTODY OF
MINORS ACT

1 The number of minor children subject to this proceeding is _____ The name, place of birth, birthdate and sex of each child, the present address, periods of residence and places where each child has lived within the past five (5) years, and the name, present address and relationship to the child of each person with whom the child has lived during that time are (See footnote)

Child's Name		Place of Birth	Birthdate	Sex
A				
Period of Residence	Address	Person Child Lived With (Name and Present Address)		Relationship
to present				
to				
to				
to				

Child's Name		Place of Birth	Birthdate	Sex
B				
Period of Residence	Address	Person Child Lived With (Name and Present Address)		Relationship
to present				
to				
to				
to				

Total Number of Continuation Pages Attached _____

* Singular includes plural. Declaration under penalty of perjury must be signed in California (CCP 2015.5). Affidavit is required when signed outside California. When declaration applies to more than two children, attach additional page (CRC 201 (b)).

Form Approved by the
Judicial Council of California
(Effective January 1, 1975

DECLARATION UNDER UNIFORM CUSTODY OF MINORS ACT

CC 5158
[8816]

For reverse side of form, see following page.

2. ☐ I have not participated as a party, witness, or in any other capacity in any other litigation or custody proceeding, in this or any other state, concerning custody of a child subject to this proceeding.

☐ I have participated as a party, witness, or in some other capacity in other litigation or custody proceeding, in this or some other state, concerning custody of a child subject to this proceeding, as follows:

    a. Name of each child:

    b. Capacity of declarant:

    c. Court and state:

    d. Date of court order or judgment (if any):

3 ☐ I have no information of any custody proceeding pending in a court of this or any other state concerning a child subject to this proceeding, other than that set out in item 2.

☐ I have the following information concerning a custody proceeding pending in a court of this or some other state concerning a child subject to this proceeding, other than that set out in item 2:

    a. Name of each child:

    b. Nature of proceeding:

    c. Court and state:

    d. Status of proceeding:

4. ☐ I do not know of any person not a party to this proceeding who has physical custody or claims to have custody or visitation rights with respect to any child subject to this proceeding.

☐ I know that the following named person not a party to this proceeding has physical custody or claims custody or visitation rights with respect to a child subject to this proceeding:

a. Name and address of person:	b. Name and address of person:	c. Name and address of person:
☐ Has physical custody	☐ Has physical custody	☐ Has physical custody
☐ Claims custody rights	☐ Claims custody rights	☐ Claims custody rights
☐ Claims visitation rights	☐ Claims visitation rights	☐ Claims visitation rights
a. Name of each child:	b. Name of each child:	c. Name of each child:

I declare under penalty of perjury that the foregoing, including any attachments, is true and correct and that this declaration is executed on (Date) . . . . at (Place) . . . . California.

. . . .

    (Type or print name)   (Signature of Declarant)

> NOTICE TO DECLARANT: You have a continuing duty to inform this court of any information you obtain of any custody proceeding, in this or in any other state, concerning a child subject to this proceeding.

[8811]

Petition for temporary custody order, see § 4600.1.

Uniform Law: This section is similar to section 9 of the Uniform Child Custody Jurisdiction Act, except that the words "as to each of the following" were added following "oath" in subd. (1), see, 9 Uniform Laws Annotated, Master Edition.

Library references
Infants ⚙︎19.1.
C.J.S. Infants § 8.

§ 5159. Additional parties

If the court learns from information furnished by the parties pursuant to Section 5158 or from other sources that a person not a party to the custody proceeding has physical custody of the child or claims to have custody or visitation rights with respect to the child, it shall order that person to be joined as a party and to be duly notified of the pendency of the proceeding and of his joinder as a party. If the person joined as a party is outside this state he shall be served with process or otherwise notified in accordance with Section 5154.

(Added by Stats.1973, c. 693, p. 1256, § 1.)

Uniform Law: This section is similar to section 10 of the Uniform Child Custody Jurisdiction Act, see, 9 Uniform Laws Annotated, Master Edition.

Library references
Infants ⚙︎19.1.
C.J.S. Infants § 8.

§ 5160. Appearance of parties and child

(1) The court may order any party to the proceeding who is in this state to appear personally before the court. If that party has physical custody of the child the court may order that he appear personally with the child. If the party who is ordered to appear with the child cannot be served or fails to obey the order, or it appears the order will be ineffective, the court may issue a warrant of arrest against such party to secure his appearance with the child.

(2) If a party to the proceeding whose presence is desired by the court is outside this state with or without the child the court may order that the notice given under Section 5154 include a statement directing that party to appear personally with or without the child and declaring that failure to appear may result in a decision adverse to that party.

(3) If a party to the proceeding who is outside this state is directed to appear under subdivision (2) or desires to appear personally before the court with or without the child, the court may require another party to pay to the clerk of the court travel and other necessary expenses of the party so appearing and of the child if this is just and proper under the circumstances.

(Added by Stats.1973, c. 693, p. 1257, § 1. Amended by Stats.1976, c. 1399, p. 6314, § 6.)

District attorney, actions to procure compliance with order to appear, see § 4604.
1976 Amendment. Added last sentence to subd. (1).
Uniform Law: This section is similar to section 11 of the Uniform Child Custody Jurisdiction Act, see, 9 Uniform Laws Annotated, Master Edition.

Library references
Infants ⚙︎19.1.
C.J.S. Infants § 8.

§ 5161. Binding force and res judicata effect of custody decree

A custody decree rendered by a court of this state which had jurisdiction under Section 5152 binds all parties who have been served in this state or notified in accordance with Section 5154 or who have submitted to the jurisdiction of the court, and who have been given an opportunity to be heard. As to these parties the custody decree is conclusive as to all issues of law and fact decided and as to the custody determination made unless and until that determination is modified pursuant to law, including the provisions of this title.

(Added by Stats.1973, c. 693, p. 1257, § 1.)

Uniform Law: This section is similar to section 12 of the Uniform Child Custody Jurisdiction Act, see, 9 Uniform Laws Annotated, Master Edition.

Law Review Commentaries
Remaining problems: Punitive decrees, joint custody and excessive modification. Brigitte M. Bodenheimer (1977) 65 C.L.R. 937.

Library references
Infants ⚙︎19.3(4).
C.J.S. Infants § 8.

1. In general
Visitation rights pursuant to stipulation modifying child custody provisions of prior dissolution of marriage decree were to be treated as "custody matters" under § 5150 et seq. Smith v. Superior Court of San Mateo County (1977) 137 Cal.Rptr. 348, 68 C.A.3d 457.

<u>Underline indicates changes or additions by amendment</u>

§ 5162. Recognition of out-of-state custody decrees

The courts of this state shall recognize and enforce an initial or modification decree of a court of another state which had assumed jurisdiction under statutory provisions substantially in accordance with this title or which was made under factual circumstances meeting the jurisdictional standards of the title, so long as this decree has not been modified in accordance with jurisdictional standards substantially similar to those of this title.

(Added by Stats.1973, c. 693, p. 1257, § 1.)

Uniform Law: This section is similar to section 13 of the Uniform Child Custody Jurisdiction Act, see, 9 Uniform Laws Annotated, Master Edition.

Library references
Infants ⚖19.3(1).
C.J.S. Infants § 8.

1. In general

Although previous order of Australian court had granted custody of parties' children to former wife and had granted former husband visitation rights, subsequent order, granting former husband custody pending further hearing of custody issue after wife interfered with husband's visitation rights by taking children to the United States, did not involve a deprivation of reasonable notice and opportunity to be heard, and, because of temporary nature of order, there was no basis for claim that Australian court intended to punish wife, and consequently Australian court order was enforceable in California. Miller v. Superior Court of Los Angeles County (1978) 151 Cal.Rptr. 6, 587 P.2d 723, 22 C.3d 923.

Where when mother commenced Illinois proceeding for modification of custody provision of divorce decree, children had lived in Illinois with either their mother or father for at least six months, Illinois was "home state" of children and on that basis Illinois court had jurisdiction to modify custody order and change custody to mother, and thus California court, which awarded custody to mother and denied temporary custody to grandfather, was compelled to recognize and enforce that order. In re Marriage of Schwander (1978) 145 Cal.Rptr. 325, 79 C.A.3d 1013.

§ 5163. Modification of custody decree of another state

(1) If a court of another state has made a custody decree, a court of this state shall not modify that decree unless (a) it appears to the court of this state that the court which rendered the decree does not now have jurisdiction under jurisdictional prerequisites substantially in accordance with this title or has declined to assume jurisdiction to modify the decree and (b) the court of this state has jurisdiction.

(2) If a court of this state is authorized under subdivision (1) and Section 5157 to modify a custody decree of another state it shall give due consideration to the transcript of the record and other documents of all previous proceedings submitted to it in accordance with Section 5171.

(Added by Stats.1973, c. 693, p. 1257, § 1.)

Uniform Law: This section is similar to section 14 of the Uniform Child Custody Jurisdiction Act, see, 9 Uniform Laws Annotated, Master Edition.

Law Review Commentaries
Continuing importance of Ferreira v. Ferreira under Uniform Child Custody Jurisdiction Act. (1974) 62 C.L.R. 365.
Remaining problems: Punitive decrees, joint custody and excessive modification. Brigitte M. Bodenheimer (1977) 65 C.L.R. 937.

Library references
Infants ⚖19.3(1).
C.J.S. Infants § 8.

Index to Notes

In general 1
Jurisdiction 2

1. In general

All petitions for modification of a custody decree are to be addressed to state which rendered original decree if that state has jurisdiction under standards of Uniform Child Custody Jurisdiction Act. Palm v. Superior Court (App.1979) 158 Cal.Rptr. 786.

Where record of proceeding on divorced mother's petition to obtain custody of her son disclosed that the trial court refused to consider evidence that would have been made available by conducting an investiga- tion into the present circumstances of the child, who was living with his father in Rhode Island, and where all that was developed at the hearing was that the mother had remarried and was able to care for both her children, that the father had moved to Rhode Island and that the boy's sister desired to be with her brother, trial court abused discretion as a matter of law in modifying the prior custody decree. In re Marriage of Kern (1978) 150 Cal.Rptr. 860, 87 C.A.3d 402.

Purpose of Uniform Child Custody Jurisdiction Act is to achieve greater stability of custody decrees and avoid forum shopping and, to that end, all petitions for modification are to be addressed to state which rendered original decree if that state has jurisdiction under the standards of the Act. In re Marriage of Schwander (1978) 145 Cal.Rptr. 325, 79 C.A.3d 1013.

Visitation rights pursuant to stipulation modifying child custody provisions of prior dissolution of marriage decree were to be treated as "custody matters" under § 5150 et seq. Smith v. Superior Court of San Mateo County (1977) 137 Cal.Rptr. 348, 68 C.A.3d 457.

2. Jurisdiction

Although under § 5150 et seq. Oregon was the "home state" of minor daughter, custody of whom had been awarded to wife in California dissolution of marriage proceeding and who had lived with her mother in Oregon for more than six months prior to institution of custody and visitation

Asterisks * * * indicate deletions by amendment

rights modification proceeding in the California divorce court, the latter court had jurisdiction to modify custody and visitation proceedings and to hold mother in contempt for violation thereof, in view of findings that child and her family had equal or stronger ties with California as compared to Oregon and that child's interests would best be served by a California forum having optimum access to relevant evidence. Smith v. Superior Court of San Mateo County (1977) 137 Cal.Rptr. 348, 68 C.A.3d 457.

Although former husband and the former wife, who presently resides in Oregon, could not confer on California divorce court jurisdiction that otherwise did not exist over subject matter of their dispute concerning child custody and visitation, from the parties' submission of visitation issue to the divorce court an inference could reasonably be drawn, for purposes of § 5150 et seq. that the parties considered the child's family and other ties with California to be stronger than her ties with Oregon. Id.

§ 5164. Filing and enforcement of custody decree of another state

(1) A certified copy of a custody decree of another state may be filed in the office of the clerk of any superior court of this state. The clerk shall treat the decree in the same manner as a custody decree of the superior court of this state. A custody decree so filed has the same effect and shall be enforced in like manner as a custody decree rendered by a court of this state.

(2) A person violating a custody decree of another state which makes it necessary to enforce the decree in this state may be required to pay necessary travel and other expenses, including attorneys' fees, incurred by the party entitled to the custody or his witnesses.

(Added by Stats.1973, c. 693, p. 1257, § 1.)

Uniform Law: This section is similar to section 15 of the Uniform Child Custody Jurisdiction Act, except that "superior court" was substituted for "[District Court, Family Court]", see, 9 Uniform Laws Annotated, Master Edition.

Library references
Infants ⚬19.3(4).
C.J.S. Infants § 8.

1. In general
Where a certified copy of Colorado custody modification decree, which modified

prior California custody decree, was filed in California court and was part of record. California, under provision of this section, was required to accord to Colorado decree same effect as if decree were rendered in California, and, since it was later in time, it superseded California custody decree which it modified. In re Marriage of Steiner (1979) 152 Cal.Rptr. 612, 89 C.A.3d 363.

2. Deposit by noncustodial parent
There was no statutory authorization for requirement imposed by trial court for a cash deposit by noncustodial mother as condition of visitation in the state of California, and expressed concern about tendency of authorities in that state to ignore custody orders from Missouri did not permit such an unauthorized condition to be imposed upon the exercise of visitation rights. Mansell v. Mansell (Mo.App.1979) 583 S.W.2d 284.

§ 5165. Registry of out-of-state custody decrees and proceedings

The clerk of each superior court shall maintain a registry in which he shall enter all of the following:

(1) Certified copies of custody decrees of other states received for filing.

(2) Communications as to the pendency of custody proceedings in other states.

(3) Communications concerning a finding of inconvenient forum by a court of another state.

(4) Other communications or documents concerning custody proceedings in another state which may affect the jurisdiction of a court of this state or the disposition to be made by it in a custody proceeding.

(Added by Stats.1973, c. 693, p. 1258, § 1.)

Uniform Law: This section is similar to section 16 of the Uniform Child Custody Jurisdiction Act, except that "superior court" was substituted for "[District Court, Family Court]", see, 9 Uniform Laws Annotated, Master Edition.

Law Review Commentaries
Remaining problems: Punitive decrees, joint custody and excessive modification.

Brigitte M. Bodenheimer (1977) 65 C.L.R. 937.

Library references
Infants ⚬19.1.
C.J.S. Infants § 8.

§ 5166. Certified copies of custody decree

The clerk of a superior court of this state, at the request of the court of another state or at the request of any person who is affected by or has a legitimate

Underline indicates changes or additions by amendment

court may issue a warrant of arrest against such person to secure his appearance with the child in the other state.

(Added by Stats.1973, c. 693, p. 1258, § 1.   Amended by Stats.1976, c. 1399, p. 6314, § 7.)

1976 Amendment. Added last sentence to subd. (3).

Uniform Law: This section is similar to section 20 of the Uniform Child Custody Jurisdiction Act, except that the provision for social studies was deleted from subd.

(a), see, 9 Uniform Laws Annotated, Master Edition.

Library references
Infants ⊂⇒19.3(3).
C.J.S. Infants § 8.

§ 5170. Preservation of records of custody proceedings; forwarding to another state

In any custody proceeding in this state the court shall preserve the pleadings, orders and decrees, any record that has been made of its hearings, social studies, and other pertinent documents until the child reaches 18 years of age. Upon appropriate request of the court of another state the court shall forward to the other court certified copies of any or all of such documents.

(Added by Stats.1973, c. 693, p. 1259, § 1.)

Uniform Law: This section is similar to section 21 of the Uniform Child Custody Jurisdiction Act, except that "18 years" was substituted for "[18, 21] years", see, 9 Uniform Laws Annotated, Master Edition.

Library references
Infants ⊂⇒19.1.
C.J.S. Infants § 8.

§ 5171. Request for court records of another state

If a custody decree has been rendered in another state concerning a child involved in a custody proceeding pending in a court of this state, the court of this state upon taking jurisdiction of the case shall request of the court of the other state a certified copy of the transcript of any court record and other documents mentioned in Section 5170.

(Added by Stats.1973, c. 693, p. 1259, § 1.)

Uniform Law: This section is similar to section 22 of the Uniform Child Custody Jurisdiction Act, see, 9 Uniform Laws Annotated, Master Edition.

Library references
Infants ⊂⇒19.1.
C.J.S. Infants § 8.

§ 5172. International application

The general policies of this title extend to the international area. The provisions of this title relating to the recognition and enforcement of custody decrees of other states apply to custody decrees and decrees involving legal institutions similar in nature to custody rendered by appropriate authorities of other nations if reasonable notice and opportunity to be heard were given to all affected persons.

(Added by Stats.1973, c. 693, p. 1259, § 1.)

Uniform Law: This section is similar to section 23 of the Child Custody Jurisdiction Act, except that the word "institutions" was deleted following the third use of the word "custody", see, 9 Uniform Laws Annotated, Master Edition.

Library references
Infants ⊂⇒19.
C.J.S. Infants §§ 7, 8.

§ 5173. Calendar priority

Upon the request of a party to a custody proceeding which raises a question of existence or exercise of jurisdiction under this title the case shall be given calendar priority and handled expeditiously.

(Added by Stats.1973, c. 693, p. 1259, § 1.)

Uniform Law: This section is similar to section 24 of the Uniform Child Custody Jurisdiction Act, see, 9 Uniform Laws Annotated, Master Edition.

Library references
Infants ⊂⇒13.
C.J.S. Infants §§ 5 et seq., 96, 99.

Underline indicates changes or additions by amendment

interest in a custody decree, shall certify and forward a copy of the decree to that court or person.

(Added by Stats.1973, c. 693, p. 1258, § 1.)

Uniform Law: This section is similar to section 17 of the Uniform Child Custody Jurisdiction Act, except that "superior court" was substituted for "[District Court, Family Court]", see. 9 Uniform Laws Annotated, Master Edition.

Library references
Infants ⊂⊐19.1.
C.J.S. Infants § 8.

§ 5167. Taking testimony in another state

In addition to other procedural devices available to a party, any party to the proceeding or a guardian ad litem or other representative of the child may adduce testimony of witnesses, including parties and the child, by deposition or otherwise, in another state. The court on its own motion may direct that the testimony of a person be taken in another state and may prescribe the manner in which and the terms upon which the testimony shall be taken.

(Added by Stats.1973, c. 693, p. 1258, § 1.)

Uniform Law: This section is similar to section 18 of the Uniform Child Custody Jurisdiction Act, see. 9 Uniform Laws Annotated, Master Edition.

Library references
Infants ⊂⊐19.3(3).
C.J.S. Infants § 8.

§ 5168. Hearings and studies in another state; orders to appear

(1) A court of this state may request the appropriate court of another state to hold a hearing to adduce evidence, to order a party to produce or give evidence under other procedures of that state, or to have social studies made with respect to the custody of a child involved in proceedings pending in the court of this state; and to forward to the court of this state certified copies of the transcript of the record of the hearing, the evidence otherwise adduced, or any social studies prepared in compliance with the request. The cost of the services may be assessed against the parties or, if necessary, ordered paid by the state.

(2) A court of this state may request the appropriate court of another state to order a party to custody proceedings pending in the court of this state to appear in the proceedings, and if that party has physical custody of the child, to appear with the child. The request may state that travel and other necessary expenses of the party and of the child whose appearance is desired will be assessed against another party or will otherwise be paid.

(Added by Stats.1973, c. 693, p. 1258, § 1.)

Uniform Law: This section is similar to section 19 of the Uniform Child Custody Jurisdiction Act, except that "state" was substituted for "[County, State]" at the end of subd. (1). see. 9 Uniform Laws Annotated, Master Edition.

Library references
Infants ⊂⊐19.3(3).
C.J.S. Infants § 8.

§ 5169. Assistance to courts of other states

(1) Upon request of the court of another state the courts of this state which are competent to hear custody matters may order a person in this state to appear at a hearing to adduce evidence or to produce or give evidence under other procedures available in this state. A certified copy of the transcript of the record of the hearing or the evidence otherwise adduced shall be forwarded by the clerk of the court to the requesting court.

(2) A person within this state may voluntarily give his testimony or statement in this state for use in a custody proceeding outside this state.

(3) Upon request of the court of another state a competent court of this state may order a person in this state to appear alone or with the child in a custody proceeding in another state. The court may condition compliance with the request upon assurance by the other state that travel and other necessary expenses will be advanced or reimbursed. If the person who has physical custody of the child cannot be served or fails to obey the order, or it appears the order will be ineffective, the

Asterisks * * * indicate deletions by amendment

Bibliography

Abarbanel, Alice. "Sharing Parenting After Separation and Divorce: A Study of Joint Custody." *American Journal of Orthopsychiatry* 49 (1979):320-329.

"Abduction of Own Child Could Result in Felony." *Los Angeles Daily Journal,* 3 March 1976.

Agopian, Michael W. "Parental Child Stealing: California's Legislative Response." *Canadian Criminology Forum* 3 (1980):37-43.

_____ . "Problems in the Prosecution of Parental Child Stealing Offenses." Paper presented at the Western Society of Criminology Conference, Newport Beach, California, 1 March 1980.

Agopian, Michael W. and Anderson, Gretchen. "Characteristics of Parental Child Stealing Offenses." *Journal of Family Issues,* in press.

Alix, Ernest. *Ransom Kidnapping in America 1874-1974.* Carbondale: Southern Illinois University Press, 1978.

Alternative Lifestyles 2 (1979): special issue on ending intimate relationships.

American Humane Association. *Highlights of 1978 National Reporting Data.* Mimeographed. Colorado: May 1979.

Amir, Menachem. *Patterns in Forcible Rape.* Chicago: University of Chicago Press, 1971.

Association of Family Conciliation Courts. *Joint Custody: A Handbook for Judges, Lawyers and Counselors.* Portland: Association of Family Counciliation Courts, 1979.

Bannon, James. "Law Enforcement Problems with Intra-Family Violence." Speech to the American Bar Association Conference, Montreal, 12 April 1975.

Bard, Morton, and Connolly, Harriet. "The Police and Family Violence: Policy and Practice." In *Battered Women: Issues of Public Policy,* pp. 304-326. Washington, D.C.: U.S. Commission on Civil Rights, 1978.

Bard, Morton, and Zacker, Joseph. *The Police and Interpersonal Conflict: Third Party Intervention Approaches.* Washington, D.C.: Police Foundation, November 1976.

Barden, J. "Wife Beaters: Few of Them Ever Appear Before A Court of Law." *New York Times,* 21 October 1974, p. 38.

Bartlett, Kay. "Child Snatching—A Family Affair." *Sacramento Bee,* 19 September 1976, p. 1.

Baum, Charlotte. "The Best of Both Parents." *New York Times,* 31 October 1976, Magazine, p. 44.

Blumenthal, Monica. "Mental Health Among the Divorced." *Archives of General Psychiatry* 16 (1967):603-608.

Bodenheimer, Brigitte. "The Uniform Child Custody Jurisdiction Act."
    Family Law Quarterly 3 (1969):304-316.
_____ . "The International Kidnapping of Children: The United States
    Approach." *Family Law Quarterly* 11 (Spring 1977): 83-100.
_____ . "The Hague Draft Convention on International Child Abduc-
    tion." *Family Law Quarterly* 14 (Summer 1980):99-120.
Bogue, Donald. *The Population of the United States*. Glencoe: Free Press,
    1949.
Bonger, William. *Race and Crime*. Translated by M. Hordyke. Montclair:
    Patterson Smith Publishing, 1943.
Bourne, Richard, and Newberger, Eli, eds. *Critical Perspectives on Child
    Abuse*. Lexington: D.C. Heath & Co., 1979.
Briscoe, C. William, and Smith, James. "Depression and Marital Turmoil."
    Archives of General Psychiatry 29 (1973):811-817.
Broustein, Sidney and Hamilton, William. "Analysis of the Criminal Jus-
    tice System with the Prosecutors Management Information System
    (PROMIS)." In *Quantitative Tools for Criminal Justice Planning,* edited
    by Leonard Oberlander, pp. 91-111. Washington, D.C.: U.S. Govern-
    ment Printing Office, 1975.
California. Assembly Bill 2549. California Legislature, Regular Session
    (1975-76).
_____ . *Civil Code, Annotated*. West Publishing, 1976.
_____ . *Penal Code, Annotated*. West Publishing, 1976 and 1977.
_____ . *Welfare and Institutions Code, Annotated*. West Publishing,
    1976 and 1977.
California Department of Justice. *Report to the Legislature—ACR 236*.
    Sacramento, California, September 1974.
Chester, Robert. "Health and Marital Breakdown: Some Implications for
    Doctors." *Journal of Psychosomatic Research,* 1973.
Clark, Homer. *The Law of Domestic Relations in the United States*. St. Paul:
    West Publishing Co., 1968.
Conklin, John. *Robbery and the Criminal Justice System*. Philadelphia:
    J.B. Lippincott Co., 1972.
Cressey, Donald. "The State of Criminal Statistics." *National Probation
    and Parole Journal* 2 (1957):230-241.
Crouch, Billie. "The Full Faith and Credit Clause and Its Relation to
    Custody Decrees." *Alabama Law Review* 11 (1958):138-158.
Currie, Brainard. "Full Faith and Credit Chiefly to Judgments: A Role for
    Congress." *Supreme Court Review,* 1964, pp. 139-158.
Demeter, Anna. *Legal Kidnaping*. Boston: Beacon Press, 1977.
Dullea, Georgia. "Parental Kidnaping: Boundaries Widen." *New York
    Times*, 29 January 1980, p. 14.
Dutton, Donald. "Domestic Disturbance Intervention by Police."

Presentation at the Symposium on Family Violence, Vancouver, British Columbia, 1977.

Ehrenzweig, Albert. *A Treatise On The Conflict of Law.* St. Paul: West Publishing Co., 1962.

_____ . "The Interstate Child and Uniform Legislation: A Plea for Extra-Litigious Proceedings." *Michigan Law Review* 64 (1965):1-12.

Fain, Harry. "1963 Proceedings." Section of Family Law, American Bar Readings in Law and Psychiatry, edited by Richard Allen, Elyce Ferster, and Jesse Rubin, pp. 316-322. Baltimore: Johns Hopkins University Press, 1968.

Fairchild, Justice of the Supreme Court of Wisconsin. Speech at the Conference of Chief Justices, St. Louis, 8 August 1961. Typewritten.

Ferretti, Fred. "2 Mellon Children Abducted Here in Custody Battle." *New York Times,* 20 March 1976, p. 1.

Fields, Marjory. "Wife Beating: Facts and Figures." In *Notes from the Women's Rights Project,* American Civil Liberties Union, 1977, p. 2.

Finkelhor, David. *Sexually Victimized Children.* New York: Free Press, 1979.

Foreman, Judy. "Kidnaped! Child-Snatching A World Problem." *Boston Globe,* 16 March 1980.

Galper, Mirian. *Co-Parenting—Sharing Your Child Equally.* Philadelphia: Running Press, 1978.

Gayford, J. "Wife Beating: A Preliminary Survey of 100 Cases." *British Medical Journal* 1 (1975):194-197.

Gaylin, Willard. *Partial Justice: A Study of Bias in Sentencing.* New York: Visage Press, 1974.

Geis, Gilbert. "Statistics Concerning Race and Crime." *Crime and Delinquency* 2 (1965):142-150

Gelles, Richard J. *The Violent Home: A Study of Physical Aggression Between Husbands and Wives.* Beverly Hills: Sage Publications, 1974.

Gil, David. "Violence Against Children." *Journal of Marriage and the Family* 33 (1971):637-648.

Goldstein, Joseph; Freud, Anna: and Solnit, Albert. *Beyond the Best Interest of the Child.* New York: Free Press, 1973.

Gore, Robert. "Child Snatching on Increase Across U.S." *Los Angeles Times,* (West Side edition) 25 May 1980.

Greenwood, Peter; Wildhorn, Sorrel; Poggio, Eugene; Strumwasser, Michael; and De Leon, Peter. *Prosecution of Adult Felony Defendants in Los Angeles County: A Policy Perspective.* Santa Monica: Rand Corporation, 1973.

Hanley, John. "Fathers Group to Fight Custody Decisions." *New York Times,* 7 March 1977, p. 57.

Hefler, Ray, and Kempe, C. Henry, eds. *Child Abuse and Neglect.* Cambridge, Mass.: Ballinger Publishing Co., 1976.

Hindelang, Michael J. "Equality Under the Law." *Journal of Criminal Law, Criminology and Police Science* 60 (1969):306-313.

————. "The Uniform Crime Reports Revisited." *Journal of Criminal Justice* 2 (1974):1-17.

Horowitz, Joy. "The Law Has Few Answers for Child Stealing Cases." *Los Angeles Herald-Examiner,* 21 March 1977.

Huey, John. "To Man Whose Job is Child Snatching, End Justified Means." *Wall Street Journal,* 24 March 1976, p. 1.

International Association of Police Chiefs. *Training Key #16: Handling Disturbance Calls.* Gaithersberg, Maryland, 1965.

"Kidnaping: A Family Affair." *Newsweek,* 18 October 1976, p. 24.

Kitsuse, John, and Cicourel, Aaron. "A Note on the Use of Official Statistics." *Social Problems* 11 (1963):131-139.

Kuhn, Mary. "There's No Place Like Home for Beatings." *Washington Star,* 11 November 1975.

Levinger, George. "Sources of Marital Dissatisfaction Among Applicants for Divorce." *American Journal of Orthopsychiatry* 36 (1966):804-806.

Lewis, Jane. "Legalized Kidnaping of Children by Their Parents." *Dickinson Law Review* 80 (1976):205-237.

Liebow, Elliot. *Tally's Corner: A Study of Negro Streetcorner Men.* Boston: Little, Brown & Co. 1967.

"Lindbergh Baby Kidnaped From Home of Parents on Farm near Princeton; Taken From His Crib; Wide Search On." *New York Times,* 2 March 1932, p. 1.

Los Angeles County District Attorney's Office. *Child Stealing Report.* August 1977.

————. *Prosecutors Management Information System: PROMIS Users' Manual.* Los Angeles, January 1977.

Martin, Del. *Battered Wives.* San Francisco: Glide Publications, 1976.

Martin, Harold, and Kempe, C. Henry. *The Abused Child.* Cambridge: Ballinger Publishing Co., 1976.

Martin, John, ed. *Violence and The Family.* New York: John Wiley & Sons, 1978.

McCoy, Meredith. *Parental Kidnaping: Issues Brief No. IB 77117.* Washington, D.C.: Congressional Research Service, 1978.

Miller, Frank. *Prosecution: The Decision to Charge A Suspect With A Crime.* Boston: Little, Brown, & Co., 1969.

Molinoff, Daniel. "Life With Father," *New York Times,* 22 March 1977, Magazine, p. 12.

Moore, Donna, ed. *Battered Women.* Beverly Hills: Sage Publications, 1979.

Morris, Albert. *Homicide: An Approach to The Problem of Crime.* Boston: Boston University Press, 1954.

National Conference of Commissioners on Uniform State Laws. *Uniform Child Custody Jurisdiction Act.* Chicago: 1968.

O'Brien, John. "Violence in Divorce Prone Families." *Journal of Marriage and the Family* 33 (1971):692-698.

Palmer, Stuart. *The Psychology of Murder.* New York: Thomas Y. Crowell Co., 1960.

Parnas, Raymond. "The Police Response to the Domestic Disturbance." *Wisconsin Law Review* (1967):914-960.

_____ . "Police Discretion and the Diversion of Intra-Family Violence." *Law and Contemporary Problems* 36 (1971):539-565.

Pittman, David, and Handy, William. "Patterns in Criminal Aggravated Assault." *Journal of Criminal Law, Criminology and Police Science* 55(1963):462-470.

Pizzey, Erin. *Scream Quietly Or The Neighbours Will Hear.* Baltimore: Penguin Books, 1974.

President's Commission on Law Enforcement and Administration of Justice. *Task Force Report: The Police.* Washington, D.C.: U.S. Government Printing Office, 1967.

"The Problem of Parental Kidnaping." *Wyoming Law Journal* 10 (1956): 225-238.

Ramos, Suzanne. "When Parents Steal Their Own Children." *New York Times,* 15 November 1979, p. 1.

"A Rationale of the Law of Kidnaping." *Columbia Law Review* 53 (1953): 540-558.

Ratner, Leonard, "Child Custody in A Federal System." *Michigan Law Review* 62 (1964):795-846.

_____ . "Legislative Resolution of the Interstate Child Custody Problem: Reply to Professor Currie and A Proposed Uniform Act." *Southern California Law Review* 38 (1965):183-205.

Roman, Mel, and Haddad, William. *The Disposable Parent: The Case For Joint Custody.* New York: Holt, Rinehart & Winston, 1978.

Roth, Allan. "The Tender Years' Presumption in Child Custody Disputes." *Journal of Family Law* 15 (1976-77):423-462.

Rounsaville, Bruce. "Battered Wives: Barriers to Identification and Treatment." *American Journal of Orthopsychiatry* 48 (1978): 487-494.

Schneider, Anne; Burcart, Janie; and Wilson, L.A. "The Role of Attitudes in the Decision to Report Crime to the Police." In *Criminal Justice and the Victim,* edited by William McDonald, pp. 89-113. Beverly Hills: Sage Publications, 1976.

Sellin, Thorsten. "The Significance of Records of Crime." *Law Quarterly Review* 67 (1951):489-504.

Selltiz, Claire: Jahoda, Marie; Deutsch, Morton; and Cook, Stewart.

Research Methods in Social Relations. Revised edition. New York: Holt, Rinehart & Winston, 1959.

Silver, Larry: Dublin, Christina; and Lourie, Reginald. "Does Violence Breed Violence? Contributions from A Study of the Child Abuse Syndrome." *American Journal of Psychiatry* 126 (1969):404-407.

Skolnick, Jerome. *Justice Without Trial: Law Enforcement in Democratic Society.* New York: John Wiley & Sons, 1966.

Smith, Dave. "Kidnaping With Impunity." *Los Angeles Times,* 19 April 1976.

_____ . "Father Outruns Law in Child Custody Case." *Los Angeles Times,* 3 August 1977.

Stansbury, Dale. "Custody and Maintenance Law Across State Lines." *Law and Contemporary Problems* 10 (1944):819-831.

Stark, Rodney, and McEvoy, James. "Middle Class Violence." *Psychology Today,* November 1970, pp. 52-54.

Steinmetz, Suzanne K., and Straus, Murray A., eds. *Violence in the Family.* New York: Dodd, Mead & Company, 1975.

Stephens, Darrel. "Domestic Assault: The Police Response." In *Battered Women,* edited by Maria Roy, pp. 164-172. New York: Van Nostrand Co., 1977.

Straus, Murray A., Gelles, Richard J., and Steinmetz, Suzanne K. *Behind Closed Doors: Violence in the American Family.* New York: Doubleday, 1980.

Uniform Crime Reports [Published Annually]. Washington, D.C.: U.S. Government Printing Office, 1978.

U.S. Code. Title 18, vol. 4, secs. 1073 and 1201-1202, 1979.

U.S. Congress. *Hearings Before the Committee on the Judiciary on H.R. 5657.* 72nd Cong., 1st sess., 1932.

_____ . *Hearing Before the Subcommittee on Child and Human Development: Parental Kidnaping, 1979.* 96th Cong. 1st sess., 1979.

_____ . *Hearings Before the Subcommittee on Crime on H.R. 4191 and H.R. 8722.* 93rd Cong., 2d sess., 1974.

_____ . *Joint Hearing Before the Subcommittee on Criminal Justice and the Subcommittee on Child and Human Development: Parental Kidnaping Prevention Act of 1979, S. 105.* 96th Cong., 2d sess., 1980.

_____ . H.R. 113, 94th Cong., 1st sess., 1975.

_____ . H.R. 1290. 96th Cong., 1st sess., 1979.

_____ . H.R. 4191. 93d Cong., 1st sess., 1974.

_____ . H.R. 4486. 94th Cong., 1st sess., 1975.

_____ . H.R. 8722. 93d Cong., 1st sess., 1974.

_____ . S. 105. 96th Cong., 1st sess., 1979.

U.S., *Constitution.* Art. 4, sec. 1.

U.S. Department of Commerce, Bureau of the Census. *Current Population*

Reports: Divorce, Child Custody and Child Support. Washington, D.C.: U.S. Government Printing Office, 1979.

_____ . *Current Population Reports: Marital Status and Living Arrangements March 1978.* Washington, D.C.: U.S. Government Printing Office, 1979.

U.S. Department of Justice. *Public Opinion About Crime: The Attitudes of Victims and Nonvictims in Selected Cities.* Washington, D.C.: U.S. Government Printing Office, 1977.

Vanderbilt, Arthur. *Judges and Jurors: Their Functions, Qualifications and Selection.* Boston: Boston University Press, 1956.

Van Gelder, Lindsy. "Beyond Custody: When Parents Steal Their Own Children." *Ms.,* May 1978, pp. 52-53.

Victimology: An International Journal 2 (1977): special issue on child abuse and neglect.

Victimology: An International Journal 2 (1977-78): special issue on spouse abuse.

Ward, David; Jackson, Maurice; and Ward, Renee. "Crimes of Violence by Women." In *Crimes of Violence,* National Commission on the Cause and Prevention of Violence. Washington, D.C.: U.S. Government Printing Office, 1969.

Warrior, Betsy. "Battered Lives." *Houseworkers Handbook,* Spring 1975. Cited in *Battered Wives,* by Del Martin, p. 255. San Francisco: Glide Publications, 1976.

Webb, Eugene; Campbell, Donald; Schwartz, Richard; and Sechrest, Lee. *Unobtrusive Measures: Nonreactive Research in the Social Sciences.* Chicago: Rand McNally Co., 1966.

Weinraub, Judith. "The Battered Wives of England: A Place to Heal Their Wounds." *New York Times,* 29 November 1975, p. 17.

Weiss, Robert. "The Emotional Impact of Marital Separation." *Journal of Social Issues* 32 (1976): 135-145.

_____ . *Marital Separation.* New York: Basic Books, 1975.

Westley, William. "Violence and the Police." *American Journal of Sociology* 59 (1953): 34-41.

Westman, Jack, and Cline, David. "Divorce Is a Family Affair." *Family Law Quarterly* 5 (1971):1-10.

White, Laura. "Women Organize to Protect Selves From Husbands." *Boston Herald American,* 22 June 1975.

Wilson, James. *Varieties of Police Behavior.* Cambridge: Harvard University Press, 1968.

Wilt, G. Marie, Bannon, James, and Breedlove, Ronald K., eds. *Domestic Violence and the Police: Studies in Detroit and Kansas City.* Washington, D.C.: Police Foundation, 1977.

Winokur, Scott. "The Child Stealers." *San Francisco Examiner,* 5 October 1980.

Wolfgang, Marvin E. *Patterns in Criminal Homicide.* Philadelphia:
    University of Pennsylvania Press, 1958.
Yankowski, Lois. "Battered Women: A Study of the Situation in the
    District of Columbia." Washington, D.C., 1975. Typewritten.
Zelba, Serapio. "Battered Children." *Trans-Action,* July-August, 1971,
    pp. 58-61.

Court Cases

Burns v. *Commonwealth,* 9 Pa. 138, 18 A. 756 (1889).
Finlay v. *Finlay,* 240 N.Y. 429, 431, 148 N.E. 624 (1925).
In re Walker, 228 Cal. App. 2d 217, 39 Cal.Rptr. 243 (1964).
Kovacs v. *Brewer,* 365 U.S. 612 (1958).
May v. *Anderson,* 345 U.S. 528 (1953).
Sampsell v. *Superior Court,* 32 Ca. 2d 763, 197 P.2d 739 (1948).
Spriggs v. *Carson,* 229 Pa.Super. 9, 17, 323 A.2d 275 (1974).

Index

Index

About the Author

Michael W. Agopian received the Ph.D from the University of Southern California in 1980. He is currently assistant professor in administration of justice at California Lutheran College, and director of the Child-Stealing Research Center. He was director of research at the Open Door Drug Clinic, from 1972 to 1973, in Alhambra, California, and evaluation coordinator for the California Department of Corrections, from 1974 to 1976, examining community-based corrections programs. As a legislative consultant he participated in creating California's parental child-stealing law and was a consultant in drafting the federal Parental Kidnaping Prevention Act. His publications appear in a variety of books and journals and include the areas of forcible rape, drug treatment, and community-based corrections.